The THIN You Within You

The THIN You *Within* You

Winning the Weight Game
with Self-Esteem

Abraham J. Twerski, M.D.

St. Martin's Press ✹ New York

Books are available in quantity for promotional or premium use. Write to Director of Special Sales, St. Martin's Press, 175 Fifth Avenue, New York, N.Y. 10010, for information on discounts and terms, or call toll-free (800) 221-7945. In New York, call (212) 674-5151 (ext. 645).

Design by Nancy Resnick

Food Guide Pyramid on pages 179 to 181 appears courtesy of the National Cattleman's Beef Association.

Library of Congress Cataloging-in-Publication Data

Twerski, Abraham.
    The thin you within you :   winning the weight game with self-esteem / Abraham Twerski.
        p. cm.
    ISBN 0-312-14433-4
    1. Overweight persons—Mental health. 2. Self-esteem. 3. Weight loss—Psychological aspects. 4. Self-acceptance. 5. Self-perception. I. Title.
    RC552.025T84   1997
    613.2'5—DC20   96-6984
                                                                                            CIP

First Edition: May 1997

10 9 8 7 6 5 4 3 2 1

Contents

Part One

Understanding Overeating

Chapter One

Why Do We Let People Insult Our Intelligence?

Every month, without fail, someone advertises a miracle diet guaranteed to reduce your weight quickly and dramatically and, as an added bonus, without starving yourself.

Let's think for a moment. If any of these phenomenal diets *really* worked, why would there constantly be a need for new and different ones? Why not just stick with the one that works? You might argue that people don't know which one is really effective, and that might be a valid argument—if the notion of dieting was recent. You could say the right diet hadn't been developed yet. However, dieting has been going on for years, month in and month out: diets, pills, exercises. Hundreds of gimmicks have been advanced over the years, and if any of these was really good, certainly it would have persisted.

It is not really accurate to say that these diets don't work. In fact, they *do* work, and that's part of the problem. Almost any diet will cause you to take off weight fairly quickly, but as most people have sadly found out, it is only a matter of time before the weight returns, and then some. The result is a yo-yo syndrome, and as some people have said, they have lost more than a thousand pounds over the years—and are still overweight.

If we were honest with ourselves, we would understand that these quick, surefire methods work for the short term, but none results in a long-term weight reduction.

Of course, if you are marooned on an island with nothing to eat but fish, you could indeed lose all the weight you wanted. But as soon as you returned to civilization, the weight would come right back. This is equally true of pills, diets, spas, surgery, and other gimmicks. None of these is sustainable over the long haul, and consequently the weight loss is short-lived.

Hope lives eternal, and each time a new promise of some magical method appears, we are vulnerable. "This time things will be different! The effects of the previous seventy-four diets didn't work, but this time I'll take the weight off and keep it off."

We know why we allow our intelligence to be insulted. We wish to deceive ourselves.

The only way to maintain a reduced weight is by a lifestyle change. We are always reluctant to make long-term changes because they can be uncomfortable. We are essentially creatures of habit. We do things a certain way, and our habits become integrated into our behavior. If you have any question about this, just transfer your wristwatch to the other hand. Even though it should not make the slightest difference on which hand it is worn, you will soon find that you are very aware of the change, and it may even feel cumbersome or awkward. Returning the watch to its usual place brings back a feeling of comfort. If feel-

4

ings of discomfort accompany so minor an alteration, how much more so with significant behavior changes? It's easy to imagine why some people consider change virtually intolerable.

Another factor in our resistance to change is an intolerance for delay. Thanks to technological advances, most tasks can be accomplished with unprecedented speed. Distances that required weeks if not months of travel can now be traversed in hours. Cooking that used to take hours can be done in minutes. Written communications that took days to arrive at a destination appear in seconds, and calculations that required laborious, time-consuming effort can be done in a fraction of a second. We have come to expect things to happen fast. However, a lifestyle cannot change at a rapid rate; it may take years. Little wonder that people who are accustomed to microwaves, fax machines, and computers are impatient with a process that takes years and are susceptible to promises of methods that take only a few weeks.

If you are one of those who have tried umpteen diets and have come to the realization that your next diet is not likely to produce any more durable results than its predecessors, this book is for you.

Much of my work as a psychiatrist has involved treatment of alcoholism. When I began working with alcoholics, a very wise and seasoned therapist told me that the only word I should avoid using with my patients was "alcohol." Recovery from alcoholism requires a lifestyle change, and as long as the focus remains on alcohol, the real problem will remain unattended. This is equally true of food, and this is one reason why preoccupation with food and diet is counterproductive: It evades the real problem.

You will therefore not find in this book much mention

of foods to eat or not to eat. Also, there is still no universal agreement on which foods to avoid or to emphasize: fat, proteins, carbohydrates. Each one has been championed or vilified throughout the years. Indeed, new and sometimes conflicting ideas about nutrition appear in the news every few weeks. How can we avoid being confused?

Obviously, we can use only the information we have, since we have no access to discoveries of the future. Furthermore, it is important to take a reasonable approach toward nutrition and not go overboard. For example, a recent finding that broccoli and spinach contain a cancer retardant does not mean that you must eat huge amounts of broccoli and spinach at every meal, but rather that these should have a place in the menu. Similarly, if it is found that a certain food may be harmful, this does not mean that it must be totally avoided. Usually the findings are based on foods fed to laboratory animals in amounts much larger than any sane person would eat.

There will always be people who champion dietary extremes, and there are many anecdotal claims for certain diets. Medical research has not confirmed any of these claims, and the reasonable approach is to have a well-balanced diet, based on the most reliable scientific information. The appendix at the end of this book contains current nutritional guidelines.

Eating problems involve two components: the person and the food. The various diets that have been unsuccessful in the long term have sought changes in the *food*. My approach is to *deemphasize the food* by avoiding fads and adhering to the general guidelines in the appendix and focusing instead on the necessary changes in the *person*. Let us now look at what some of these are.

Chapter Two

Just What Is
an Eating Problem?

When does eating become an "eating problem"?

The primary function of eating is to provide the body with its necessary nutrients. This function, in its purest form, is best observed in animals in their natural habitat. Animals in the wild are not obese or bulimic. When their nutritional needs are satisfied, they stop eating.

This situation in human beings is not as simple. Over and above its nutrient value, food has social and ritual values. Various religious services include eating or drinking, and many social activities center around food. "Breaking bread" together has symbolized friendship since ancient times. Although we may have met all our daily nutrition requirements, partaking of hors d'oeuvres at an evening reception can hardly be considered an "eating problem."

Eating that results in overweight can be both a physical and emotional problem. Ideal body weight cannot be calculated to the ounce. If the normal range for a person is 140–145 pounds, we hardly consider her obese if she weighs, say, 147 pounds. Although there is no precise demarcation between healthy and unhealthy weight, bear in mind that the heart was designed to serve the ideal weight efficiently, and that each additional pound adds *almost a mile* of blood vessels, which places an additional workload on the heart. It is also known that overweight contributes to high blood pressure and to metabolic diseases, such as diabetes. From a health perspective, maintaining the ideal weight is desirable, and if eating results in excess weight, it may be considered a "problem."

Eating can be an emotional problem when it is "compulsive," when you feel compelled to eat even though you intellectually understand that you should not be eating and aren't even hungry. You may *think* you are hungry, but you know that this desire for food is not in your body's best interest and yet you feel driven to eat.

Bulimia is a compulsive condition in which one feels compelled to eat and then compelled to lose weight. Some people consider being slender as attractive and think themselves overweight even though they are well within or even below the normal range. Their preoccupation with food, in quest of an idealized image rather than the physiologically ideal weight, results in their eating habits becoming a "problem."

Elsie is a thirty-year-old woman who is representative of many others. At 5´3˝, and given her frame, her ideal weight should be plus or minus 116 pounds. However, at 115 pounds Elsie considered herself to be fat. She periodically dieted and exercised to lose weight and fluctuated between 110 and 118 pounds. Her moods varied with her weight, but it was difficult to determine which was cause and which was effect. Much of her waking time was occupied with ruminating about food, about her weight, and about her wardrobe. This preoccupation had far more to do with her self-image than with health considerations. While there was nothing grossly abnormal about Elsie's behavior, she was generally unhappy, except for those days when she weighed 110 pounds, and her unhappiness could certainly be considered to be a "problem."

Some people have an "average" ideal weight if calculated over an extended period of time, but the average is a result of a yo-yo pattern, alternately gaining and losing weight. This apparently healthy "average" is misleading. For example, a room at a steady seventy-degree temperature is comfortable. Wide temperature fluctuations between sixty degrees and eighty degrees yield an average of seventy degrees, but we would hardly say that the room was generally comfortable.

There are several studies that demonstrate that compulsive eating and especially bulimia are more prevalent among women than men, and that there has been a significant increase in bulimia since the 1980s. It cannot be mere coincidence that this period coincides with some fairly radical changes to the female role in society.

Several writers have pointed out that for all the gains achieved by the feminist movement, there have also been some severe stresses. Stereotyping has its limitations and may indeed be oppressive, but broadening horizons and increasing one's options is not without cost.

In 1968 I was asked to develop a counseling service for Catholic nuns, some of whom were thrown into turmoil by the liberal changes of Vatican II. One thirty-five-year-old nun who had served as a teacher since entering the convent came for a psychiatric consultation, bringing with her a questionnaire she had received that asked about her interests and what she would like to do in the next several years. In addition to the traditional roles of the nuns as teachers or nurses, there were now opportunities for a variety of positions in community services. The nun threw the questionnaire on my desk and stated angrily, "If I wanted to have a choice of careers, I would not have entered the convent. I used to receive a little card telling me where I was assigned to do the Lord's work. I don't want to make choices."

To some people, being dictated to may appear tyrannical, but to someone who does not want the responsibilities of decision making, this is a desirable arrangement.

The "traditional" female roles of homemaker, teacher, secretary, nurse, or social worker may indeed have been stifling to women whose creativity was suppressed, but there was relatively little stress in choosing a lifestyle. A woman who chose the role of wife and mother had no reason to feel that she was performing a less than optimum role. Today, however, with the opening of professions and business opportunities to women, the choices are much wider, and the demands of some of the available roles are much greater. To add to this, women in the workplace often feel that they have to prove that they are equal to or superior to their male counterparts. A woman may feel that she has to choose between being a wife and mother or being a doctor, lawyer, or executive. Choosing the former may result in her feeling that she is not fulfilling herself and that resigning herself to the traditional role is a regression, whereas choosing the latter frustrates her maternal instincts. She may therefore decide to do both, which results in what Dr. Harriett Braiker has termed the "type E woman," the "E" meaning "everything to everybody."

Men are generally not subject to being type E, and although a man may have a type A personality—being time-driven, constantly under pressure to meet deadlines, relentlessly striving for success, intolerant of delay, and overassertive—he does not have as much need to vindicate himself as the woman does, nor is he expected to perform full time at home. The type A professional or executive may indeed have a harrowing day at the office, but when he comes home, it is perfectly acceptable for him to kick off his shoes and recline in the lounge chair.

Not so for the woman, who may end the "workday" with feelings of guilt that she has abandoned her children to a latchkey existence, and who, rather than recline in an easy chair, must prepare dinner, review the children's school activities, and prepare the children's clothes for the following morning, to name just a few of her duties as a homemaker. Furthermore, it is not enough that she meets the "minimum daily requirements" that might be adequate for the traditional homemaker. This woman must prove that her homemaker's duties are not being adversely affected by her career, and vice versa. One career woman said, "Being type A would be like a vacation."

A thoughtful, considerate husband may ease the woman's conflict and help her fulfill both roles, but not all husbands understand the wife's dilemma, and not are all up to providing the necessary support.

Time may eventually clarify the roles and ease the challenges for the woman of the future, but today's woman is caught in the period of transition. To further complicate things, many women who seek to compete with their male counterparts have been brought up with concepts of femininity that conflict with the aggressive behavior they must adopt to make their place in professional or commercial circles. In short, today's woman may find herself subject to contradictory demands.

Some psychologists claim that compulsive eating symbolizes the conflicting roles that confront the modern woman, with eating representing the passive, nurturing mother, and the slimming representing the aggressive, competitive masculine identity. Others say that the slimming represents compliance with society's standards of what is sexually attractive, while excessive eating represents a rejection of the social norms. While there may be some truths in these formulations, both are simplistic.

There is no denying, however, that the modern woman is caught in an identity conflict, which in itself can depress self-esteem or aggravate preexisting low self-esteem. While men are also subject to various stresses and conflicts, there is a preponderance of self-concept stress in the modern woman, which may explain the much higher incidence of eating disorders in women as well as the rise in the incidence of these conditions in the past few decades.

What choice should a woman make, and how should she go about making her choices? When a woman behaves according to other people's expectations, instead of fulfilling her own needs or desires, the result is often stressful. What is needed, then, is for a woman to identify what her own needs are and to feel that it is permissible for her to satisfy them. But before a woman can identify her needs, it is important to understand the compulsion behind her eating habits, whether they are consistent overeating, yo-yoing, or bingeing and purging.

Chapter Three

Why Willpower Doesn't Work

As we have seen, compulsive eating means uncontrollable eating, because that is what a compulsion is: A person feels compelled to do something that she does not want to do. Something has taken over an aspect of her behavior so that she must do a particular act. In obsessive-compulsive disorders, this is often some type of ritualistic behavior. For example, one of my clients could not get to sleep at night unless he placed his shoes in a "T" formation under his bed. He knew this made no sense, but he was helpless to fight it. He tried numerous times to leave his shoes any which way, but finally he had to comply in order to get to sleep. In compulsive eating, the ritual manifests itself in eating more than one should or bingeing.

Some people consider compulsive eating to be a failure to exert willpower. They think that if you simply set your mind to it and made a more sincere, dedicated effort, you could avoid overeating. They see compulsive eating as a weakness of character, as laziness, and as an unwillingness to put forth the effort.

This is true only if you consider it a failure of willpower to pick up a pan from the stove and, finding that the metal handle had been exposed to the direct flame, drop the pan. Why didn't you exert some willpower and hold on to the pan? So what if it hurt? Weren't you aware that dropping the pan would cause all the food to go to waste as well as dirty the floor? I doubt that there is anyone sufficiently stoic to hold on to a burning hot handle, and certainly we wouldn't criticize anyone who dropped the pan for not using willpower.

Hindus who are expert at yoga are said to be able to lie on a bed of sharp nails. Shall we conclude that anyone who removes his or her hand from a sharp object to avoid being injured is a morally weak person who is lacking in willpower? In these instances we understand that the discomfort may be so great that it is unrealistic to expect a person to exercise willpower and withstand the pain. We need only to understand that the discomfort of the compulsive eater may be so great that willpower alone cannot overcome it.

The reason for the often-heard assertion that "only a recovering alcoholic can treat another alcoholic" is that someone who has not personally experienced the compulsion to drink may not be able to understand it and may consider the recourse to alcohol as a failure to exert willpower. The same may be said of the compulsive eater's desire to eat, which may be so intense and forceful that unassisted willpower is inadequate to resist it, much as the pain of a burn compels a person to drop a hot utensil.

The classic resolution "I'll quit tomorrow" is doomed. After a binge, when a compulsive eater is temporarily free of the compulsion, she sincerely believes that she will be able to control the desire to eat next time around. All past experiences notwithstanding, she does not recognize the true nature of the compulsion and sees the problem as a willpower issue. This misconception results not only in failure to seek competent help with the problem but also causes the person to castigate herself for her failure to exert her willpower.

The expectation of being able to control everything is part of modern life. It may well be that prior to the era of mechanization, the issue of control was not as dominant as it is today.

Think of it this way. In the days of the horse and buggy, one steered the horse by pulling on the reins, but tugging on the rein did not actually *control* the horse. Rather, the tug on the rein caused the bit to irritate the horse, which turned or stopped to relieve the pain. The horse was essentially given an offer it could not refuse. Theoretically, if the horse was starved and saw a pile of hay, its hunger might override the pain, in which case it might head for the food rather than do what the rider wanted.

This changed when the car replaced the horse. When you turn the steering wheel, you are not telling the car what you want it to do; you are in absolute control of it. This was not possible with the horse.

When I was a child, I had a little truck that I pushed across the floor, and a wind-up tractor that traveled on its own but could go only in a straight line. Today I walk into a room and see a little vehicle running around every which way, under direction of a four-year-old child who is sitting at the other end of the room, gleefully operating an electronic control panel. At this tender age, the child is learning that he can control things, even remotely. Growing up in the age of electronic marvels, he will have abundant experiences in controlling things, as when he sees his mother calling their home telephone from the department store and activating the oven to begin cooking supper.

When the *Explorer II* satellite was on the fringes of the solar system, some *two billion* miles from Earth, I watched on television how it was responding to a command from the space center. I felt the chill run up and down my spine when I realized that we have the ability to control things that are literally at astronomical distances from us.

The technological age has so imbued us with a capacity to control that we assume that there must be something dreadfully wrong if we are unable to exert control. We may perceive the inability to control our behavior as being a character deficit, and since this is an insult to our ego, we do not admit that control is impossible and continue to act as though we had control. This may explain the repeated attempts at dieting, even when experience has shown us that it simply does not work.

Let me make something clear. We are always responsible for our behavior, and lack of control does not exonerate us from such responsibility. This is not at all a contradiction.

One recovering alcoholic with many years of sobriety put it this way, "Inside the brain there are control centers for everything, with automatic shutoff mechanisms when the body has had enough. There is one for alcohol, and when that functions well, the person has one or two drinks and does not want any more. My automatic control for milk is perfectly intact, and I never have more than one glass of milk a day. My automatic control mechanism for alcohol was on the blink, but I didn't know that. When people told me that I was drinking too much, I didn't know what they were talking about. When I hit my rock bottom and realized that I was out of control, I wanted to stop, but with the automatic being on the blink, I didn't know how to use the manual control. What the AA program did for me was to teach me how to use the manual."

If the automatic regulatory mechanism is nonfunctional, then all we need to do is to learn how to operate manual controls. We cannot engage in destructive behavior and claim that we are not culpable because the automatic regulatory system is not operating properly. The good news is that the concept of "irresistible impulse" is nonsense. We *can* change our behavior.

Let us assume that some people have a faulty regulatory mechanism governing food. If they accept this as an unfortunate fact of life and direct their efforts at learning how to implement manual control, they can overcome their compulsive eating. If they refuse to obtain help and proceed to try to activate the nonfunctioning automatic system because they perceive its dysfunction to be a sign of character weakness, they will spin their wheels as they are dragged downward.

There are indeed ways of gaining control, and this is what recovery is all about, but progress toward this goal cannot begin until you face the fact that your automatic regulatory system is on the blink.

Have you ever been in the embarrassing position of your host asking you whether you enjoyed the gnocchi, only to discover that you didn't even taste it because you gobbled it down so fast? It is ironic that people who eat excessively, who might be thought to be savoring the taste of food, may actually fail to fully enjoy it because they are too busy eating it.

Have you ever been consumed with anger because your boss berated you and was unreasonable in his demands, even though you were the one who kept the office from being totally chaotic? And on returning home, you

17

tried to drown your wrath by eating a half gallon of ice cream, only to find that now you were both angry and sick, and you wondered why on earth you did that, vowing to never be so foolish again?

Have you ever determined that this was *it*, that you'd had it with overeating, then that very night went to a Weight Watchers meeting, came home enthused with your commitment to lose weight and begin the diet *tomorrow*, and decided that since the dieting begins tomorrow, you are entitled to one last fling, and you eat a whole bag of cookies?

In retrospect, all these incidents of excessive eating appear foolish, and a reasonable person with a respectable IQ should not be acting in such a grossly irrational manner. But that is in retrospect, applying omniscient hindsight. At the moment you ate, it seemed like the proper thing to do. Why?

Dieting to control weight generally fails, probably because it is an attempt to apply logical thought to eating problems. Obviously, weight gain is directly related to consuming more calories than are used, so what could be more logical than to reduce or alter the food we eat? The pitfall here is that we are trying to apply logic to a condition that is independent of logic and that may even exist in stark defiance of logic.

Compulsion occurs when we feel compelled to do something *against* our will. The source of the compulsion may be irrational, but because we respect our conscious mind and pride ourselves in being rational people, we are unable to accept that we are acting illogically and so find explanations for our behavior. In effect, we rationalize to conceal the true reason for our actions, or sometimes we are simply unaware of the real reason, and since we are uncomfortable acting without explanation, we come up with a plausible reason.

Rationalizations are very common. We all rationalize at one time or another, giving ourselves fairly plausible explanations for what we do. Rationalizations are nothing but attempts to give ourselves plausible reasons to cover up for the *true* reasons, which are often *unconscious* reasons.

In psychology, there is a concept of "unconscious motivation," which means that you may have an urge to do something but are not aware of why you want to do it, or even that you want to do it at all. It is as though you are being manipulated to do something, much like a puppet's movements are manipulated by the puppeteer who pulls the strings. We say that the motivation to do this particular act comes from the unconscious mind.

The mind consists of two components, the conscious and the unconscious. The conscious mind contains things of which we are aware, and the unconscious mind is the storehouse of all our past experiences. For example, you may not be able to recall the names of any of your classmates in the second grade, some thirty years ago, even if you are ordered to do so at gunpoint. Yet one night, for no apparent reason, you have a dream about several of your second-grade friends, and you address them by their names. Where was this information all the time? It was in your unconscious mind. Then why couldn't you retrieve it? Because that is what the unconscious mind is: *not* conscious, or beyond your awareness.

Sigmund Freud suggested that the unconscious mind is not only a storehouse of memories and feelings but is also dynamic; that is, the ideas in the unconscious mind can cause you to act, but since the ideas are not in your awareness, you may do things without knowing why. In fact, if the pressure of an unconscious idea is stronger than the conscious will, you may even do things that you do not want to do. This is what is meant by unconscious motivation. It is like having a "puppeteer" within you pulling the strings.

Freud was helped to his theory of unconscious motivation by a demonstration he witnessed. In an effort to enhance his knowledge and technique of hypnosis, Freud attended a lecture by Dr. Liebault, who was an acknowledged authority in the field. Liebault hypnotized a member of the audience and suggested to him that at some time after he returned to his seat, he would stand up and open his umbrella. He added the suggestion that he would not have any recollection that he was told to do so, which is a fairly typical posthypnotic suggestion. After Liebault terminated the trance, the man returned to his seat and Liebault continued with his lecture.

After a bit, the man abruptly stood up and opened his umbrella, standing there quite stupefied by this strange act. Liebault asked the man why he had opened his umbrella inside the room, and the man could not explain why he had done so. Liebault asked whether anyone had instructed him to do so, and the man replied negatively. Liebault kept pressuring the man that there must be some reason for his act, but no matter how much he pursued the issue, the man denied any knowledge of having been instructed to do so and could not give any reason for his action.

Freud observed that this man had done something quite unusual and had no inkling why he had done so. How could he obey an instruction of which he had no knowledge? Freud concluded that the instruction to open his umbrella was indeed in the person's mind even though he was not aware of it, or was not *conscious* of it. There must therefore be an area of the mind that is a repository of ideas that can motivate behavior, of which the person is oblivious. This "compartment" of the mind is the *unconscious*, and the demonstration convinced Freud that contrary to most people's belief that we always do things for apparent, logical reasons, there are some things we do because of unknown and seemingly illogical reasons. In other words, we may act as a result of *unconscious motivation*.

Carl was a successful accountant who came for treatment because of an annoying compulsion. Whenever he sat down at the table to eat, he had to get up and change chairs. He could not continue to sit at the first place he assumed.

As we went through his history, Carl recalled that when he was eight or nine years old, his grandfather visited them and took the chair at the head of the table usually occupied by his father. Carl then took his usual place at the table, but his mother said, "Get up from there. That's your father's place." About twenty years later, the young man began feeling uncomfortable when he sat down to eat and felt that he had to change places. He continued to do this for a number of years, until he decided that this was senseless and that he should get treatment to get rid of it.

The whole explanation for this act is complex, but to simplify it, it involved a conflict that Carl had with his mother, who had disapproved of the woman he was going to marry. He felt guilty for defying his mother's wishes in marrying her, and the ritual of changing of the chairs was his symbolic way of obeying his mother's wish, a command that she had given him many years earlier. By getting off his chair, which his mother had at one time told him to do, he was trying to compensate for disobeying her in the marriage.

21

This is the power of compulsion. It makes little difference whether the compelling notion is a command given under hypnosis, or any other motivation that lies hidden in your mind. If there is a force compelling you to act, you may be unable to resist it, and fighting the urge may exact an extraordinary amount of anxiety.

I cite these examples to clarify two points about a compulsive urge: It usually is extremely powerful and almost irresistible; and the act often appears totally illogical. You may not wish to do it, and you may intellectually understand that you should not do it, yet you are virtually helpless to resist.

If the compulsion to eat has these characteristics, we can easily understand why a person who consciously is determined to lose weight is not able to resist the urge to eat and why logical approaches to weight loss are inadequate.

Let us see now what kinds of forces are involved in the compulsion to eat.

Chapter Four

Compulsive Eating: A Self-Esteem Deficiency Problem

Compulsive eating is a product of a complexity of factors. Rather than being due to a single cause, it is much like a recipe, where no single ingredient results in a cake. Furthermore, even several ingredients together do not yield a cake, and the final product is not forthcoming unless all the necessary ingredients are there in proper proportion.

People are subject to various types of discomfort. There can be physical pain, as from an injury, or emotional distress, such as depression or irritation. Whereas physical pain is often due to a single cause, the "recipe" that results in emotional distress is often a combination of genetic, physical, social, psychological, and environmental factors. For example, people who work for a company that is downsizing may be concerned about their job security, yet various employees react differently to this threat. A person who has physical health, self-confidence, a supportive family, and a generally upbeat outlook may feel much less threatened than a person who has health problems, emotional insecurities, a fragile marriage, and a negative outlook on life. The latter may become quite depressed by the specter of possible job loss, and this depression may even result in her being unable to perform her work adequately, thus aggravating her insecurity.

Eating and weight problems are also likely to be the result of a number of factors in combination. There are physical factors, with some people supposedly having more "fat storage cells" than others, or a slower metabolism. Some people can eat heartily, including desserts, yet not seem to put on weight, whereas another person of the same height and build, whose habits are not any more sedentary than the first, readily gains weight from eating a fraction of the other person's intake. Not all metabolic workings have been elucidated, but there do appear to be some metabolic differences among people. Social, environmental, and psychological factors also play a part in the final outcome.

Some things are not changeable, such as one's genes. At this point in medical science, whatever genes you have, you are stuck with. So as far as physical factors are concerned, with the exception of thyroid malfunction there does not appear to be much we can do about metabolism. Social and environmental factors, such as your job, living arrangements, friends, and neighbors, are changeable, but making such changes is generally of little value in altering how you feel or behave. Moving from one area to another, the "geographic cure," has a poor track record for alleviating an eating problem, nor can you successfully cure an eating problem by getting out of a marriage. This leaves the factor most readily changeable and probably the one that plays the most important role in the recipe: psychological.

We can make significant changes in how we think and

feel, and correcting this ingredient and thereby removing it from the recipe can successfully relieve an eating problem, and do so over the long term. One of the most important feelings in this regard is *self-esteem*, and I have found that many people do not have self-esteem. Rather, they harbor unwarranted feelings of inferiority and inadequacy, which are distressful in themselves and also give rise to a number of unpleasant feelings and maladaptive behaviors.

All people are unique. We know that among billions of people no two individuals have identical fingerprints, and that absolute identity of a person can be made on the basis of fingerprints. Personality is even more unique than fingerprints, and there are no two people in the world—not even identical twins—who are completely alike in intellectual, emotional, and psychological makeup. While there are enough similarities among people to allow us to assume that a medication that works for many people will be effective for a new patient, it is not at all uncommon to find that the new patient does not respond to the medication and must be looked at as an individual rather than as one of a group. This is particularly true in psychotherapy, where the differences in psychological makeup render each person unique. Nevertheless, some generalizations can be made.

One of the unpleasant feelings that is at least partially caused by lack of self-esteem is what I call "anxiety," and this unpleasant sensation is a common factor in compulsive eating. Generally, we think of anxiety as stemming from fear, but in fear there is always a catalyst—something of which we are frightened. In anxiety there is no known catalyst. If you are driving down an icy hill and you lose all control of your car, you experience fear. Your heart beats fast, you gasp for air, your chest tightens, and you have a feeling of impending doom. This emotional and physical reaction is perfectly understandable given the circumstances. If, however, you are standing in the checkout counter of the supermarket or driving on an uncrowded highway on a pleasant sunny day and you suddenly have similar feelings, this is usually referred to as anxiety, because there is nothing to justify these feelings.

In my lexicon, such feelings should be termed *panic* rather than anxiety. I like to use the term *anxiety* to refer to a vague feeling of displeasure, which is not necessarily accompanied by any of the other symptoms of panic. Nor is anxiety the same as the feeling of sadness that occurs in depression. Anxiety is a feeling that defies precise description and may be best described as, "I feel lousy." *Lousy* never made it into the legitimate psychological terminology, so the term cannot be used in respectable writing. We therefore have to borrow the respectable term, *anxiety*. It means to be ill at ease, often with no idea why or what to do about it. "I feel lousy" provides no avenue to alleviate the feeling by removing its cause, since its cause is generally unknown.

Having self-esteem means having a good self-image, a feeling that you are worthy, likable, and competent. (I elaborate on this important feeling in the chapters that follow.) People with self-esteem are more likely to adjust to the various challenges and stresses in life without developing anxiety, whereas a lack of self-esteem renders a person much more vulnerable to anxiety.

Anxiety or feeling lousy, which is often due to poor self-esteem, can be a very, very unpleasant sensation, often virtually intolerable, and people try to escape this misery in a variety of ways. Some ways are constructive, as when we are stimulated to accomplish things that give us a good feeling. Other ways are neutral, such as reading or watch-

26

ing television. But some methods are frankly destructive, such as eating in order to feel good or using excessive alcohol or drugs.

Why do some people choose one method of escape rather than another? Various theories exist, but no one can say for certain what determines the choice of escape.

Even some constructive escapes are not without drawbacks. Certainly a person who eliminates anxiety by increasing her efforts at profitable work is doing something positive, yet the fact is that she is being motivated by a negative rather than a positive emotion. Since she has not eliminated the source of her anxiety, she is likely to feel lousy again once she has achieved the goal she set for herself, and her only recourse is to set and pursue another goal. This can result in workaholism, which may have negative consequences such as a lack of attention to one's family and to spiritual matters, or may lead to physical problems such as migraines, peptic ulcers, high blood pressure, and coronary artery heart disease.

The effect of alcohol and chemicals is fairly obvious: They render the mind oblivious to unpleasantness—at least temporarily. Since the effect is brief, the person is likely to continue using these chemicals, with a high risk of addiction.

Many people get relief from anxiety by means of food, even though they have already eaten enough to have satisfied the body's nutritional needs. There may be different ways food brings about this sense of relief, perhaps by causing the brain to release endorphins, similar to the mechanism of chemicals.

A psychological explanation has been offered that may be valid. Probably the very first sensation of anxiety that we experience in life is hunger. When an adult who has not eaten for a while feels hungry, she is not likely to confuse the sensation of hunger with anxiety. However, the infant cannot make such a distinction, and to the infant, hunger *is* anxiety. When he or she is fed, the hunger anxiety disappears. These are the earliest life experiences and are repeated many times in infancy, so that the young mind is impressed that *food can relieve anxiety.*

This, then, is how the unconscious mind may handle anxiety in later life. It remembers how anxiety was repeatedly relieved by food during infancy, and even though there is no longer any logic to this connection, it continues to operate. The body's demand for relief may result in the command "Eat!" and this command has the force of compulsion. The fact that the person is unaware of why she is eating and of the origin of the compulsion makes no difference. The fact that these processes take place in the unconscious portion of the mind does not in any way diminish their force.

An infant whose mother's primary response to her cry, no matter what the origin, was promptly to stick a bottle in her mouth has a greater vulnerability to develop compulsive eating habits. It is probably true that mothers who are themselves anxious and insecure know of only one response to a baby's cry: feed it. Mothers who feel better about themselves and are not threatened by a baby's crying may be the ones whose children have a healthier attitude toward food. These are oversimplifications, because eating problems are not caused by the presence or absence of a single factor. Nevertheless, the notion of early parental response may lend some insight to the adult's attitude toward food.

While early life impressions are important, they are by no means the only experiences that influence a person's relationship with food. Furthermore, even if we know how some attitudes originated, this knowledge does not automatically result in our being able to change them. We may know that the cause of a fire was a match that ignited it, but blowing out the match does nothing to extinguish the flame. Similarly, knowledge of how and why psychological reactions came about may not do much to change them, and the only practical application of such knowledge is preventive. If we know the origin of our problems, we can try to avoid causing these problems in others, especially in our children. However, once a life pattern has been established, we need to find other ways of undoing them than by historical analysis. Let us now look at some of these ways.

Chapter Five

The Role of the Self-Image

Evelyn came for a consultation accompanied by her husband. They had been married for nine years and had one child. Evelyn was employed as an office manager in a legal firm and was most efficient at her job. She was an excellent homemaker, and her husband spoke about her in superlative terms. She was attractive and intelligent. Her husband was flabbergasted when Evelyn broke down crying several days earlier and confided that she had been living a "double life." She said that she was really a "crazy" person and had kept her insanity a secret from him because she loved him and was afraid he would leave her if he ever found out.

Evelyn's "insanity" was bulimia. She binged and then forced herself to throw up. Sometimes she took large doses of laxatives to purge herself. She had done all this secretly, sometimes while her husband was asleep, sometimes at work. She occasionally disappeared after a meal, making some excuse for her absence, terrified that her husband would discover the truth. "I'm so terribly ashamed. But it's too much. I can't keep up this act any longer."

Evelyn's husband put his arm around her and assured her that he loved her. He did not understand why she was acting this way, but he would be helpful in any way he could.

"You don't need a crazy wife," Evelyn wept. "You deserve something better."

Evelyn's history was fairly typical of many bulimic women. She had been an excellent student and had many friends in high school. At about age sixteen she became very concerned about her weight, although it was not above the normal range. There were several girls in her class who were much thinner, and Evelyn had been envious of them. She tried to lose weight by dieting, but this did not work, because she became hungry and then ate. She reasoned that if she could not control her eating, she could get rid of what she had eaten, and thus began the pattern of eating and regurgitating, eventually developing into secretly bingeing and purging.

Evelyn's bulimia had begun with a feeling that is not uncommon among young women: I am not attractive. I need to be thin to be more attractive. This was a gross misjudgment, because Evelyn was indeed quite attractive by most people's standards—except her own.

We all have a self-concept, an idea of how we appear to others, and this is based on what we think of ourselves. We usually assume that whatever we see is reality, and that other people perceive reality the same way we do. For example, if I see a tree before me, I have no reason to believe that this is a hallucination and that there is no tree there. I assume that everyone sees the same tree that I see.

Similarly, if I have an idea of what I am and what I look like, I assume that this is reality, and that everyone who sees me sees what I see in myself. If I think I am unattractive, then I believe that everyone who looks at me sees an unattractive person. If I think that I am dull, then anyone who meets me sees the dull person I am.

The fact that people are in fact attractive and bright does not preclude their thinking of themselves as ugly and stupid. When a person thinks negatively of herself, she cannot have self-esteem. To her, the negative self is the reality, it is the truth, and the way she lives is based on this faulty assumption.

Absence of self-esteem is found in every eating problem, whether compulsive eating or bulimia. Every person with an eating problem may be thought to have two "selves," the real self, which is factual, and the fantasy self, which is the distorted image the person has of herself.

Lack of self-esteem can contribute to an eating problem in a number of ways. In Evelyn's case, she imagined herself to be unattractive, and her quest to be thin set in a pattern of eating and bingeing. Thinking poorly of oneself often results in feelings of insecurity, as when one anticipates failure or rejection, and this may result in feelings of anxiety that are sometimes, at least temporarily, relieved by food. The woman whose compulsive eating results in overweight, or who binges and purges, feels worse about herself because of her eating problem. We thus have a self-reinforcing vicious cycle. The eating problem, which had its origin in a distorted self-image with feelings of inferiority, results in further self-deprecation, which intensifies the negative self-concept.

You might think that all that is necessary to relieve a negative self-image is to point out the facts to the person, to show her that she is indeed attractive, competent, and likable. Unfortunately, this is not enough. Evelyn's husband had often told her that he loved her, and at the office she was considered to be extremely competent, but the factual knowledge had little impact. How we think of ourselves cannot be overcome by factual information alone.

Once a pattern of compulsive eating gets started, it may take on a life of its own. In other words, it had its origin for one reason but begins to serve other purposes along the way. Sometimes the original reason is no longer operative, yet the problem continues because of subsequent reasons.

An example of this is Annette, who was an overweight compulsive eater. She said that her compulsive eating began because of boredom after she had her first child and was home alone all day with the baby. She found that nibbling was relaxing, and eventually she put on excessive weight. When the child was four, Annette enrolled her in a day care program and went back to work as an executive secretary. Her day was no longer boring, but the compulsive eating continued. Several attempts at dieting were futile.

Annette said that she very much wanted to lose weight. "People don't like you if you're fat. They don't invite you to parties and things like that," which is, of course, the way she saw things. Annette had a very poor self-image and had assumed that she was not a likable person and that people would not desire her company. She had felt this way as long as she could remember, even as a child. She expected that she would not be invited by people, but since the thought "I am not likable" was so distressful, her psychological defense system caused her to think, "People are avoiding me not because I am not likable but because I am fat."

In the *Peanuts* cartoon strip, Peppermint Patty repeatedly gets poor grades. Rather than consider herself to be a poor student, Patty thinks of herself as having a big nose, and this is why her teacher gives her failing grades!

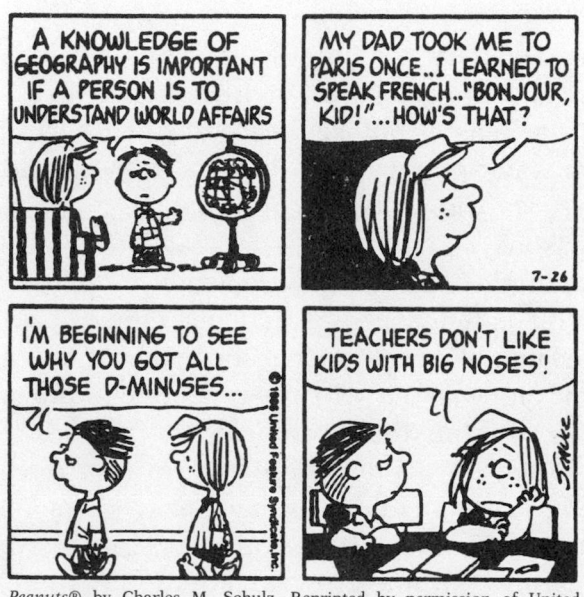

Peanuts® by Charles M. Schulz. Reprinted by permission of United Feature Syndicate, Inc.

For Annette, thinking herself to be unattractive because she was overweight was much like Peppermint Patty diverting her attention from her schoolwork to her facial features. Annette would not have to feel that she was a bad person, only that she was fat, and second, she always had the option of losing weight and thereby making herself more likable. The weight gain, which originally came from boredom, was being perpetuated because it served another purpose. It is characteristic that behavior that begins for one reason comes to satisfy other emotional needs.

Think of it in this way. Suppose that because you plan to write a book, you buy a personal computer to use as a word processor, to facilitate your editing and frequent revising. If not for this reason, you would have gotten along very well without a computer. Then you discover that it is really much more effective than a typewriter to write letters and other documents, because it is so much easier to correct typographical errors. You also find that it is great for keeping track of your checks, bills, budgets, and income tax data. Then you discover that it is a wonderful file for your recipes, and also that once you enter all the names and addresses for your greeting card list, it is just a matter of moments instead of hours to print out all the labels.

Eventually you finish the book you were writing, and you really have no more need for the word processor function, which was why you bought the computer initially. However, you would not give it up now for all the tea in China, because it serves so many other valuable functions.

This is what may happen with any particular behavior. It initially comes about because of reason A, but once it is there it happens to serve reasons B, C, D, and E. Even if reason A later disappears, the behavior remains because it has come to serve other functions. This is what psychologists mean by "overdetermination of a symptom"; the behavior is determined by more than one factor.

Compulsive eating may serve more than one function. It may initially start as tranquilization for a particular type of anxiety, but then it is found to serve some other functions. Therefore, even if we could analyze away or eliminate the initial cause, the behavior now has a life of its own, since it serves other functions in the person's psychologic economy.

The reason why a true self-awareness and the development of self-esteem can be so effective in overcoming compulsive eating problems is that many of the other factors—B, C, D, and E as well as A—may *all* be consequences of the distortion of the self-concept, and when that is corrected, all of the factors fueling the compulsive eating may be eliminated, which then permits long-term maintenance of the ideal weight.

Like Annette, most people who have two "selves"—the real self, who they *really* are, and the fantasy self, who they *think* they are—haven't the faintest idea that this is their situation, because they are convinced that the fantasy self is in fact the real one! This lack of awareness of the real self and the mistaking of the fantasy self for the real self can result *in all kinds of maladjustments to life*.

For example, Connie had a distorted self-image. Her parents were opposed to her choice of a husband, and even her friends asked what in the world she saw in John, who was far inferior to Connie in intelligence and personality. While others saw that Connie was making an improper choice, Connie's decision was based on what she thought of herself, and as far as she was concerned, someone like John was what she deserved.

Connie developed a dependency on tranquilizers and came into treatment for this. As the treatment gradually helped her come to a better self-awareness, Connie began to realize the disparity between herself and John and that they were really incompatible. Connie had made an important decision in her life, an erroneous one, on the basis of her distorted self-concept.

Bertram was an obese young man who was extremely passive. His inability to assert himself resulted in people taking advantage of him. One time he bought an appliance that was defective, but he didn't take it back to the store because this was too much of an assertion for him. He often became very frustrated because of his lack of self-assertion, and then ate to soothe his frustration. Bertram's inability to assert himself was a direct consequence of his poor self-image. He did not feel secure enough to stand up against anyone.

If people are asked whether they have an accurate self-knowledge, if they know who and what they really are, most insist that they do and are likely to reject any suggestion to the contrary. My clinical experience has shown me, however, that many people who are sure that they know themselves actually have little inkling about their true selves.

I have found it quite difficult to convince people that their self-perception is faulty, even when I present them with strong evidence to that effect. I have discovered that, strangely enough, some people adhere to a delusion about themselves more tenaciously than to the facts.

I once gave a demonstration of hypnosis to our hospital staff, and Carol, one of our secretaries who had been successfully treated by hypnosis for a severe skin condition, volunteered to be the subject. I wanted to show the staff that one could suggest hallucinations. I put an empty chair next to Carol and told her that when she opened her eyes, she would see her friend Martha sitting beside her. Upon opening her eyes, she turned to the empty chair and carried on a lively conversation with her hallucinated friend.

I then noted that Martha was sitting in the audience, and it occurred to me to try an experiment. I had Carol close her eyes, and I motioned to Martha to sit beside Carol so that Martha was on her left and the empty chair was on her right. I then instructed Carol to open her eyes, and she again turned to the empty chair and talked to the fantasy friend. I walked to her left and called her, and when she turned to her left and saw her friend there, she appeared startled and looked from her left to her right and back again. "How can Martha be in both places?" she asked.

I said, "Carol, I am playing a trick on you. Martha is in only one place, and the other is a hallucination. Now I want you to look at both Marthas very closely and tell me which is the real one."

Carol looked alternately to her right and left several times, then pointed to the empty chair. "*This* is the real Martha," she said.

Clearly it is possible to believe the fantasy person one thinks herself to be as more factual than the real person that one is.

Okay, there is the real you and the fantasy you. The real you, the one that is adequate and competent, is the one that has the automatic control system that shuts off the hunger sensation when the body's nutritional needs have been satisfied. The fantasy you is a make-believe person, one that exists only in your imagination. This fantasy person does not have a shut-off mechanism that is part of a normal physiology, and it is this fantasy person that resorts to food for relief of the stress and causes you to feel hungry even when you are nutritionally satisfied. It is this fantasy self that is giving you the command to eat, and because you believe the fantasy self to be real, its demands appear to you to be real, demands you must obey.

Some people who have irrational compulsive thoughts and urges try to get rid of them by pushing them out of their minds. Unfortunately, compulsive thoughts are much like a coiled spring. If you try to get a spring out of the way by pushing it down, it only increases in force and pushes back harder against you. In fact, the harder you try to compress it, the more force of recoil you generate. This is what is so frustrating about obsessive-compulsive thoughts. Trying to get rid of them can be counterproductive. Similarly, when you try to overcome the urge to eat by dieting, the urge may become stronger and more irrestible.

Ideally, we should reach into the depths of the mind and get rid of the origin of these pesky thoughts, but that is easier said than done. If the thought was implanted by hypnosis, the solution is relatively simple: Rehypnotize the subject and remove the suggestion. With spontaneously occurring compulsive thoughts it is much more difficult to remove the command.

In most cases of compulsive overeating, while the solution is not as simple as with a hypnotically induced compulsion, it is not a terribly complex problem either. We often are able to identify the origin of the thought as the fantasy self that is giving you the command: "Eat! Eat!" What you must do is *get rid of the fantasy self*. You must recognize your real self, which will without doubt elevate your self-esteem. This is why I titled this book *The Thin You Within You*. It is the erroneous notion of inferiority that we have of ourselves and that comprises the fantasy self that so often results in compulsive eating.

How can you find your real self? Step one is to recognize that in fact there *is* a fantasy self. This itself can be of some help. I have heard some alcoholics who had auditory or visual hallucinations say, "I know I see it, but I know it's not there," or "I can hear this voice telling me to do things, but I know it's crazy." While many people believe what they are seeing or hearing, some have insight even in their intoxicated state that their experience is imaginary.

A person who believes a hallucinated monster to be real may jump out the window to escape it or try to fight with it. Recognizing the hallucination to be unreal may eliminate such destructive behavior. One woman who was suffering from alcohol-induced hallucinations sat quietly in her chair and said, "I can see one hundred cats all over the room, but I know they are not there," and she did not try to chase them out. I once came into a room of a patient who was hearing voices due to his drinking, and I heard him shouting, "You're not real, you're not real!" He explained that he was hearing voices calling his name and telling him to jump out the window, but he knew these were hallucinations. Just the awareness that there is a fantasy self that has no existence in reality may be of some help, because one does not need to obey a command that is being given by a nonexistent being. If you can be aware that the urge to eat is due to an order being given by a source that does not exist in reality, it may be a bit easier to resist it.

But this is obviously not enough. What is needed is to get rid of this fantasy self. This is totally different from letting the fantasy self hang around and trying to ignore its command to eat, which is like pushing against a coiled spring. Those who believe in possession by demons may try to get rid of the unwanted inhabitant by exorcism. What must be accomplished psychologically is somewhat analogous to exorcism—find a way to rid of this troublesome fantasy self and clear up this confusing two-in-one state. When this is accomplished, you are who you really are, and the *real* self is thin.

Chapter Six

Why Do We Have
a Fantasy Self?

I'm going to tell you something that may surprise you. If you have a fantasy self, you are by no means alone, not even in a minority. I dare say that 99.9999 percent of people in the world have a fantasy self!

A newborn infant does not enter the world with a sophisticated concept of himself or herself. The idea of self develops as the people around us tell us who and what we are. Primarily, of course, there are our parents, but many other people also influence us. They tell us we are male or female, what race we are, what religion we are, and eventually everything else about ourselves. They tell us if we are good or bad, heroic or cowardly, bold or shy, liked or disliked, good-looking or unattractive, fat or thin. By the time we begin to think for ourselves, we already have a self-image, one that was put partially together for us by others.

Katherine is a twin, and her father showed obvious preference for her sister. She remembers her father saying, "You're not like your sister. You're goofy." Katherine could not understand why her father had this opinion of her, because she had better grades in school and had as many friends as her sister did. Although she could not see any factual reason for her feelings of inferiority, being put down by the father caused her to feel bad about herself.

Many things can happen in early childhood to contribute to a negative self-concept. First, we come into the world as little, helpless infants and are surrounded by people who appear to us to be powerful giants. This initial impression of relative inferiority may well be the root of a negative self-image. When a sibling comes along and parental attention is diverted, this may cause a child to feel that she is less loved than the baby. If a sibling is sick or has special needs that require more parental care, this may also be misinterpreted by a child. Failure to show affection, which may be caused by the parents' preoccupation with work or other distractions or may be the result of the parents' difficulty in being emotionally demonstrative, may be perceived by the child as an indication of her being unlovable. Parental discord, alcoholism, and certainly abuse may result in the child concluding that she is somehow bad. A young child may develop an erroneous negative self-concept that lingers throughout life.

Some people who "hid in the broom closet" as children never outgrow this feeling, and they continue to "hide" as adults. One may be even out in the open yet still be hiding.

Although Katherine is an attractive young woman with a charming personality, she is essentially a recluse. Her life consists of her job and hibernating in her apartment. She is fearful of dating, expecting rejection because she is unlovable. The idea that she was less likable than her twin sister persisted into adulthood. When she could not avoid gatherings, such as at family events or at office parties, she would walk the corridors or hide in the restroom.

As children we developed a pattern of getting to know ourselves through what other people told us, and there is nothing to make us think that this method of self-awareness is unreliable. We may continue on through life taking our cues from others, and we may constantly seek out other people's impressions to tell us something about ourselves. Just as we continue to walk for the rest of our lives on the basis of how we learned to walk in infancy, so we may continue to assess ourselves according to what others think about us, or at least how they *seem* to think about us as demonstrated by their actions. We are very unlikely, say at age twelve or thirteen, to stop and say, "Maybe I'm really not the person I think I am. Maybe the impressions I was given about myself are incorrect. Maybe I should set all these impressions aside and begin from scratch, trying to figure out for myself who I am and what I really want to be." This can hardly be done in adolescence, and even when we reach adulthood we are not likely to embark on an identity search until some crisis compels us to do so. Yet even as adolescents we have already been subject to pressures from society and peers, which may cause us either to reinforce the identity we have developed in childhood or to reject it in favor of another one *that our culture wishes us to have*. In one way or another, our self-image is imposed on us from without, and this is how we continue throughout our lives until we take steps to correct our self-image.

Karen came into therapy because of "severe anxiety." She was an only child, and her father was an alcoholic who was abusive to her. Her mother always took her father's side, and when Karen was an adult, her mother explained, "I agreed with him in order to placate him, because he would drink more if he was irritated." Her mother's explanation came fifteen years too late, because as a child of an alcoholic father and a mother who did not defend her, Karen felt herself to be a bad person.

Karen had put herself through nursing school and had taken a job with many responsibilities. Her anxiety occurred because she felt inadequate to the demands of her work. She was unsure whether she was performing adequately, and the staffing at the hospital was so skimpy that her superiors simply did not have time to supervise her. "I have always needed someone to validate me. I must have someone tell me that what I am doing is right, otherwise I assume that I am doing something wrong."

During her evaluation, it became evident that Karen was a compulsive eater and went on crash diets to lose weight. I pointed out to her that her current crisis was actually a blessing in disguise, because it revealed that she had been functioning with a markedly depressed self-esteem.

Part of our identity also results from molding ourselves according to the wishes of our parents, who are usually the most profound influences on our self-image. There may be others—siblings, grandparents, uncles and aunts, teachers and friends—who all let us know who we are and, even more important, *who they think we should be*. Since most of us have a strong desire to be liked, we tend to act in ways that will achieve this perfection. We become what other people want us to be. These influential people in our lives may have varying wishes as to what they would like us to be, and it is quite possible that these wishes will conflict. This results in a serious dilemma: We have to be different things to different people, unless we can construct a personality that is acceptable to everyone, which is no small feat. While all this is going on, from childhood onward, there is one thing we may be overlooking. *What would I want to be if it were left only to me?* What if I was like Adam in the Garden of Eden? Would I be the person I am now? Most people never think that. The reality is, of course, that we are not Adam in the Garden of Eden, but rather one of several billion people on Earth, a member of a culture, community, and family, with whom we would like to get along amicably. A truly independent self-evaluation rarely occurs.

But what if, just what if, this part of us that is "Adam" cries out to be itself and is repeatedly stifled. We might never even get to thinking about what this "self" might be. But if, as I suspect, "Adam" is within us and desires expression, and we push him back like a jack-in-the-box and keep the lid on tightly, the situation becomes tense. The fact that we constantly have to push him back down can drain our energy.

There is not only tension but, more specifically, anger. Imagine being cramped into a tight enclosure, banging with your fists and shouting, "Let me out!" That sounds like a very angry cry, and if my thesis is correct that this is the real self within us that wants to express itself but is being suppressed, there must be many angry people walking around.

Among the patients I have seen in thirty-five years of

46

psychiatric practice, many were frustrated and angry because they had not been able to fulfill themselves, having been forced into a mold by others' expectations. This feeling of anger at being suppressed can be very hard to pinpoint and is very poorly defined, because not knowing just what is going on makes it difficult to feel angry. Anger is usually felt at or toward someone or something, and if you don't know who or what you're angry at, the feeling doesn't come out as anger but rather as a vague although intense feeling of lousiness or anxiety. It is this feeling that drives us to do many things we hope will give us relief, and that includes eating.

It should be noted that if we could gently and slowly open the lid and let the jack-in-the-box emerge gradually without an explosive appearance, the tension could be relieved. If "Adam" could come out into the open and be his own person, the anger at being cooped up and stifled would disappear. The real self would then take the place of the artificial fantasy self.

The emergence of the real self does not mean that one comes out of the shell and does whatever one wishes and to hell with the world. Giving free rein to all our impulses—or at least to everything we can get away with—sounds more like an animal than like a dignified human being. While being whatever everyone else wants us to be is undesirable at one extreme, being a wild animal is undesirable at the other extreme.

Marilyn was twenty and in her second year of college, and although she was actually making good grades, she abruptly left school. Several months later she consulted me at her father's insistence. She had been defiant of "hypocritical bourgeois values" and was going to follow the dictates of her own conscience. In the process she had left home, lost a valuable semester from school, become pregnant and had an abortion, and been beaten by her boyfriend.

Being one's own self means exercising one's reason and judgment in establishing values, goals, and lifestyle. It means listening attentively to what others have to say, and after thoroughly deliberating, coming to our own conclusion about what to do with our lives. We must consider what it is to be a human. Would it have been appropriate for Adam in the Garden of Eden to behave like any other animal, or is there some higher goal, a loftier purpose to human life? These are all considerations we must weigh carefully and come to a concept of ourselves as individuals. Indeed, we are individuals living in society and relating to other people, but individuals nonetheless.

It is this self-awareness that can permit the emergence of the real self and send the fantasy-self packing. Attaining such self-awareness is hard work, and many people choose the easy way out.

ONE GOOD THING ABOUT
BEING A NOBODY IS THAT
YOU NEVER HAVE TO WORRY
ABOUT HAVING AN
IDENTITY CRISIS...

Assuming you are a nobody may be the easy way out, but is certainly not the best way. The Talmud tells the story of a traveler who asked a child for directions to the city. The child said, "There is a short way that is a long way, and a long way that is a short way." The man chose the short way and soon found himself at the outskirts of the city, but the entry paths to the city were blocked by private properties that were enclosed by high fences. He retraced his steps and then took the long, more arduous path, which eventually brought him to his desired destination.

Most people make it through life without ever having a true self-awareness. They take the short road and in fact are not even frustrated at not arriving at their destination because, come to think of it, they never really had a destination. It is often only when some life crisis forces us into a self-awareness that we begin to think more seriously of "who am I" and "what am I for," and if we seize this opportunity, we can come to a true self-awareness. Reaching the crisis stage in an eating problem can provide such an opportunity.

The story about the short path and the long path is certainly appropriate to eating problems. The quick-fix path is the short one that is the long one, because you must retrace your steps. Unfortunately, you may try another short path or any number of short paths before realizing that to get to the destination you must take a longer and more difficult route, but if you persist and have patience, you finally do arrive.

Part Two

The Problems
of Overeating

Chapter Seven

Anger

As we have seen, eating problems may occur when food is used to alleviate emotional discomfort. A frequent source of such discomfort is *anger*, an emotion that often presents difficulties. Perhaps it is an overstatement to say that the path to the refrigerator is paved with anger, but most compulsive eaters readily admit that they have difficulty managing their anger, and that anger frequently triggers a binge.

This is only part of the story. This reaction is in response to the anger they are *aware* of. There may also be feelings of anger a person is completely *unaware* of.

When an idea or an emotion is "too hot to handle," our psychological defense apparatus may relegate it to the unconscious part of the mind and try to keep it out of our awareness. This mechanism is referred to as "repression" and is often utilized to conceal feelings of anger from ourselves.

There are various reasons why we repress anger. Some

people have little or no faith in their controls, and they are afraid that if they allow themselves to feel angry, they will act out their feelings with violence. This is especially likely to occur in someone who was raised in a home where there was overt violence, either physical or verbal. To them, anger and violence are inseparable, and they are so frightened of becoming violent that they turn off all angry feelings. Others have been led to believe that anger per se is evil and sinful, and that decent people never feel angry. Still others are concerned that any manifestation of anger will alienate people from them, and they are desperate in their need to have people like them.

Controlling or consciously suppressing the expression of anger is not the same as repression. In suppression we know that we are angry, but we consciously decide not to react. For example, if you are provoked by your employer, you may consciously suppress an angry reaction to preserve your job. But repression means that you do not even *feel* the anger, and this is as dangerous as not feeling pain when pricked by a sharp object.

I had as a patient a nun who suffered from chronic depression, which had been resistant to all treatment. I saw her once a month. She did not drive, so she had to take several buses to come to the office, which took more than an hour.

One time I had to leave town abruptly, and somehow I neglected to call the nun, who showed up for her appointment. After waiting a long time she was told I had left town.

When I returned and discovered my dereliction, I called her and apologized and arranged for another appointment. When she came I again apologized for my failure to notify her of my absence, and said, "You must have been very angry with me, having made that long trip and spent time in the waiting room only to discover that I wasn't here."

"Oh, no," she said. "I wasn't angry at all."

"That can't be true. You wasted more than a half day because of my failure to notify you, and that would make anyone angry."

"I wasn't angry," she repeated. "I realize how things like that can happen. You are a very busy man."

"I'll do my own apologizing," I said. "It is only appropriate for you to be angry, and if you wish, you can accept my apology and get rid of the anger."

"But I wasn't angry at all," she insisted, smiling sweetly.

This is what is meant by repression. The nun had been taught that anger is sinful, and this was so deeply impressed upon her that she was unable to feel legitimate anger for fear that it was evil to do so.

Just as there is a scientific principle that matter and energy can neither be created nor destroyed, so it is true that anger cannot be destroyed by repression. It lurks in the unconscious, continually seeking ways it can gain expression. It requires energy to maintain repression, which explains why it is possible for you to feel utterly exhausted even though you have not had any physical exertion.

Just as compulsive eaters may resort to food to assuage conscious feelings of anger, they may do so in response to unconscious feelings of anger, the difference being that in the latter case they are unaware of why they are bingeing, feeling only the compulsion to eat.

Anger, like pain, has an important function, although both are distressful. Pain is a signal that something is affecting our physical system that may be injurious to us. If there were no pain, we might have a ruptured appendix or a heart attack without being aware of the critical situation. Similarly, anger is a signal that something is wrong, particularly that *some injustice is occurring*. We may be angry if we feel that we are being treated unjustly; even if we are not personally involved, we may be angry when we see an injustice being done to others. If there were no such thing as anger, we might stand idly by while atrocities were being committed against other people.

Anger is largely dependent on our values, on what we consider just or unjust. We generally consider a personal injury to be unjust. Yet although we do not like it, we do not get angry at the dentist when he or she causes us pain. It is thus not the pain that causes us anger, but the feeling that we are being hurt without cause. If someone accidentally steps on our toes, this pain may elicit an initial feeling of anger, the injustice being the person's carelessness.

When anger is a reaction to an actual injustice, it can be constructive by motivating us to correct things. If our sense of values is distorted and we consider things unjust even when they are proper, anger can be destructive. We are therefore wise to analyze our anger before reacting to it. Furthermore, even when anger is justified, we can react constructively or destructively.

There are several stages of anger. In order to avoid confusion, let us define terms, so that we know which phase of anger we are talking about.

An initial feeling of anger occurs when we are hurt, offended, or provoked in any way. This is an automatic response, almost of a reflex nature, and there is relatively little we can do about it. Since we do not have a choice whether or not to feel this anger, we cannot assign any moral value to it. We cannot say that it is wrong to feel the initial anger, any more than we can say that it is wrong to feel pain when pricked with a sharp instrument. I use the

56

term "anger" to refer to this initial reflex *feeling*.

We do have a choice as to *how we react* to this initial feeling. We may decide to bite our tongue and not react at all, or to say something to whomever provoked us, or shout, or hurl expletives, or strike out physically. There is a broad spectrum of possible responses ranging from none to violence from which we can choose. I use the term "rage" to refer to the *reaction* to anger. Rage can vary from very mild to very intense.

After feeling the initial reflexive anger, we may let go of it or we may hang on to it, perhaps waiting for the moment when we can take sweet revenge. Hanging on to the anger is also a matter of choice; hence we can assign a negative value to it. I use the term "resentment" to refer to the *persistence* of anger after it is initially evoked.

Note that I said that there is relatively little we can do about the initial feeling of anger. This is not the same as saying that nothing can be done about it. The little that can be done is that we can set our personal thermostats so that we are a bit less sensitive to provocation. It is similar to the degree of sensitivity of our skin. A sharp object applied to a thick, calloused area may not produce much if any pain, whereas just a slight touch to a sunburned area can cause much pain. Our emotional makeup may vary from "calloused" to "sunburned." A person with low self-esteem is much more sensitive to a slight than someone who feels good about herself and so may be more easily provoked to anger.

It is also understandable that we are more sensitive to the actions of some people than to others. If someone in my family, particularly someone on whom I feel dependent, says something offensive to me, I feel this much more keenly than a similar comment made by a stranger. By the same token, we are far more concerned about reacting to anger (rage) against someone close to us than to a stranger. Inasmuch as we are likely to have much more frequent contact with family members than with strangers, it is obvious that difficulties with all phases of anger are more commonly encountered with those people we love the most.

We are most offended when we feel deprived of something we deserved. If you do your job only mediocrely and are not given a raise, you do not feel offended. However, if you perform with excellence and feel that you were passed over, you may feel very angry. Anger is related to what we think we deserve, and we may feel outraged when we think that an injustice has been done to us.

Thus, if we see that others appear to be enjoying the world a great deal more than we are and have a greater share of worldly goods, we may feel that life is unfair, and we may be angry with specific people, with society as a whole, or with God. The feeling that life is unfair is often a cause of bingeing.

Most people have been raised with concepts of fairness. It is not cynical to acknowledge that much that goes on in the world is not fair. There is nothing fair about a tidal wave, a flood, or an earthquake. There is nothing fair about one person winning a huge sum of money in a sweepstakes while others win nothing. Whereas in some interpersonal relationships we have a right to expect at least a measure of fairness, we must realize that there are many unexplainable things in the world that do not follow the principle of fairness, and if we do not have unrealistic expectations, we will not be so upset when "unfair" things happen. Of course, the term "unrealistic" is relative. Just because we think something is perfectly realistic doesn't mean that everyone sees things in the same light.

Grace had never refused her sister-in-law's call for help.

Many times she had taken care of the kids when Sandra and her husband went on vacation. She had put herself out for Sandra on many occasions, and it had not happened that she needed a favor in return, until her father-in-law became seriously ill and Grace wanted to accompany her husband to visit him. Grace asked Sandra to look after their four-year-old during her absence, but Sandra said she had other commitments. Grace was furious, and that night binged, which she had never done before.

Grace did not ask Sandra what her "other commitments" were. Perhaps they really did prevent her from taking care of Grace's child. Sandra may not have been the ungrateful person Grace thought her to be. Grace certainly thought that what she asked of Sandra was realistic, whereas Sandra may have seen it as unrealistic, and possibly for valid reasons.

A person may feel so inferior and be so guilt-ridden that she considers herself undeserving of anything, and she may accept unfairness as her just deserts. In such instances, a person may allow herself to be victimized and not feel the anger she should be feeling, because she does not perceive the situation as being unjust. It takes careful analysis to determine what is just and what is unjust. Since our judgment of what is just or unjust may be skewed by our feelings, it is helpful to get an objective opinion from an unbiased outsider. Discussing things with a friend or clergyman, for example, is often very helpful. When I served as a rabbi, I helped a number of people who were making no efforts to improve their lot in life because they felt they deserved nothing better.

Angry responses occur along a wide spectrum. A newscast tells us about a person who was so embittered by the loss of his job that he went on a murderous rampage and killed several people at his former workplace. This is a result of a psychotic level of sensitivity, a gross distortion of judgment, and a total absence of restraint. Far, far removed from this is the person who binges on food because of a personal insult by her employer. But as widely different as they are, both share a common factor of being improper responses to anger.

Emotions can grossly distort our thoughts and make us oblivious to reality. Resentments, in particular, can have such a blinding and distorting effect. If you have a resentment against someone, nothing he or she does appears right, and you may misinterpret everything as being an expression of hostility toward you. These distortions lead you to believe that the other person is being provocative, which elicits further feelings of anger and resentment.

One drug addict who had multiple imprisonments for drug-related crimes was again imprisoned for robbing a drugstore. This time his mother was counseled not to pay his bail, and he eventually came to our rehabilitation center. When asked why he was in jail, he answered, "Because my mother did not hire a lawyer to get me out." For three weeks he was totally unable to see that his imprisonment was due to his holding a gun to the pharmacist's head. The resentment against his mother blinded him to the reality of his own behavior.

Here are just some of the thoughts that can result in anger and resentment.

- I have often been treated unfairly.

- I wouldn't have so many problems if other people treated me better.

- I can't stand it if someone lies to me.

- It really upsets me if someone snubs me.

60

- Someone who behaves badly should be punished.

- It really ticks me off if things don't go the way I planned.

- What happens to me usually depends on luck.

- I've had so many unfair things happen to me in my lifetime that I'll never get over them.

- There is no good excuse for breaking a promise.

- If I have to ask my wife/husband/child/friend/lover for a favor, it's not really worth having.

- If people really care about me, they'll know how I feel about certain things without having to be told.

- If someone hurts me in some way, I have the right to get even.*

There are some ways we can manage anger and resentments. First is to stop placing blame on others for whatever goes wrong. We should realize that much of the time we are probably at fault when things go wrong. For example, if someone standing at the edge of a cliff is blown over by a gust of wind, he may be angry at God for bringing about the wind, but by standing at the edge of the cliff he placed himself in a vulnerable position. Before faulting others, we ought to look closely at what we ourselves may have done to contribute to the unfortunate incident.

We must also relinquish the notion that we deserve bet-

*From *Of Course You're Angry* by Gayle Rosellini and Mark Worden. Copyright © 1985 by Hazelden Foundation, Center City, MN. Reprinted by permission.

ter and that the world should operate according to the principles of fairness. If our expectations are realistic, we are not likely to be disappointed and easily angered. We all have our own agendas and are looking out for our own betterment, not everyone else's. It is indeed wonderful when people are considerate and sacrifice their own comforts and convenience for others, but it is a mistake to expect this and then be disappointed when our expectations are not met.

It is a bit more difficult to apply this kind of thinking to those we love. We do expect husbands and wives, brother and sisters, parents and children to set aside their own desires for one another, and this does often occur. But even here it is wise to lower our expectations and understand that a person's desires may so influence his thinking that he does not realize that he is being inconsiderate. If we were totally honest with ourselves, we would have to admit that we have occasionally placed our personal interests and desires above those of someone we love, perhaps being unaware that we have done so. For example, a husband who loves his wife may be so involved in a business transaction that he forgets their wedding anniversary, and the wife is hurt and angered by this, taking it as an indication of his lack of love for her. The husband may regret this omission, but the reality is that his interest in his business distracted him from something that was indeed important to him. We can understand why the wife feels hurt and angry, but if she understood that it is possible to be distracted and that forgetting even something as important as a wedding anniversary does not indicate a lack of love, her anger would be much less intense.

A good rule to live by is to judge others as we would like to be judged ourselves. If we are honest and straightforward, we will recognize that we too have inadvertently made errors of commission or omission, where we had no bad intent whatsoever. It is only proper that we give others the same consideration we would like given to us.

It is important that anger not lead to an automatic, reflex response. As intelligent people, our behavior should be processed through the highest level of intellect and be submitted to critical, rational thinking rather than be allowed to emerge from the lower levels of the brain, those that we have in common with animals. The idea of counting to ten before reacting to anger is indeed wise, but a time delay itself is not sufficient. During this delay we should try to consider what the anger is all about. Why am I *really* angry? What do I expect to accomplish with my response? There is no validity whatsoever to the concept that venting one's anger, whether by screaming or throwing things, helps dissipate it. Such behavior may actually intensify the anger, as well as give us a reason for regretting our foolish actions and feeling guilty about them.

I have noted that anger usually occurs when we feel there has been an injustice. If we are angry at ourselves, it is because we feel that we have committed an injustice. Anger at oneself is thus identical with guilt.

The comparison of guilt with physical pain should enable us to understand that just as there is pain for which there is no demonstrable cause, there can also be guilt for which there is no evident reason. Such feelings of guilt are pathologic, and a characteristic of pathological guilt is that it cannot be relieved by any of the mechanisms that are effective for normal guilt. Neither confession nor amends nor penance can eliminate pathological guilt; it generally requires psychological or psychiatric treatment. People suffering from clinical depression often have profound feelings of guilt, sometimes even being obsessed by some "unforgivable sin." Careful questioning and analysis of the history reveal that there are no valid grounds for these guilt feelings. When the depression is relieved, whether by antidepressant medication or psychotherapy or both, the feelings disappear.

The reaction to anger can be constructive or destructive. If an injustice has indeed been done and we communicate our displeasure appropriately, we can bring this to the attention of the parties involved. This may lead to rectification of the injustice. If we react with fury, we undermine the efforts of our communication and accomplish nothing.

© Lynn Johnston Prod., Inc. Reprinted with permission of Universal Press Syndicate.

I once treated a business executive for anxiety-induced chest pain. In the process, I discovered that he was tyrannical at the office and terrorized his staff with his outbursts of rage when things were not done the way he wanted. I pointed out to him that the substance of his message was probably valid, but that most of the content was lost because his employees became defensive when he began screaming and just tuned him out. Using relaxation techniques, he was able to bring his rage under control, and his meetings at the office became much more productive. One time when I called to change an appointment, his secretary said, "Whatever you are doing with him, please keep it up. We are getting more accomplished here than ever before, and he's a pleasure to work with."

Effective communication skills are important in dealing with ourselves as well as with others. If we are displeased with something we have done and can examine it calmly, we may be able to discover why we made a mistake, what factors led to it, and how to avoid repeating the mistake. If we react to our mistakes with rage, we may be so consumed by the reaction that we are unable to analyze what we did and why, and we are likely to repeat the mistake, resulting in even greater rage at ourselves.

Remember that rage is a reaction to anger. If you turn to food to assuage your anger, you are essentially behaving in rage. Seeing it this way, eating, even very calmly and quietly, can be considered a rage reaction and is invariably counterproductive to the initial anger. Now add the anger at having eaten too much, and you are off on a vicious cycle.

There are times when we become angry because of actual injustices that are done, either against ourselves or against others. If we do not react reflexively with rage, our better judgment can prevail and we can respond constructively. The most common cause for inappropriate reaction, whether rage or sulking, is hurt pride. An oversensitive ego can distort our judgment.

Many years ago I assumed the position of assistant

rabbi to my father. I was young, with a fair amount of book learning but no experience. When I had to officiate at a funeral for the first time, my father asked me if I had prepared the eulogy. I said yes. "Would you like to review it with me?" he asked.

I felt the blood rush to my head. My feeling was, "No. I would definitely *not* like to review it with you. If you don't have trust in me, then you should not have taken me as your assistant. If you think I am capable of holding the position, then you don't have to check whether my eulogy is good enough."

Fortunately, I said, "I wrote it out and left it at home. I'll go get it if you wish" (in fact I had it in my pocket). "Please do," my father said.

I went home and told my wife how angry I was that my father had no trust in me. She said, "You're being silly. You can either learn by mistakes or by being taught by someone who has had experience. Telling you that you still have something to learn when you are new on the job does not mean he doesn't trust you."

My wife was obviously right, and I understood the value of being taught rather than learning by mistakes. My resentment abated a great deal, but the wisdom of my wife's words notwithstanding, I still felt hurt and still took it as a kind of mistrust of me. What an ego!

When I read the eulogy to my father, he pointed out to me that there was a bitter rift among members of the family of the deceased, and some of what I was planning to say could be misinterpreted by some of the family as an affront against them. He suggested that I eliminate one sentence, which I of course did.

This is an example of the sensitivity of pride and the problems that can result from such increased sensitivity. Here my father was loving and caring, trying to help me avoid a costly mistake, yet my response to this was resentment instead of gratitude! Only as I matured did I come to appreciate his guidance.

Resentment instead of gratitude! As absurd as this sounds, it is nonetheless a fact. Some of the anger that paves the way to the refrigerator may have its origin in a person's inability to accept helpful guidance.

The human ego makes its appearance at a very early age, and even children have a sense of pride, which they guard zealously. If you have ever asked a child to say "I'm sorry," you have seen the resistance this often elicits. The child may be ready to do anything except apologize. Why? Because to admit that one was wrong is perceived as an insult to the ego, and children, no less than grown-up rabbis, are often unwilling to admit that they were wrong.

Hanging on to resentments is self-defeating. After all, the person whom we continue to resent is not affected negatively by how we feel toward him or her. *We* are the ones who suffer from retention of anger, since it can result in migraine headaches, high blood pressure, ulcers, and of course, compulsive eating. Why punish ourselves when it is this other person who has been unjust to us? As one person aptly put it, "Harboring resentment is like letting someone you don't like live inside your head rent-free!"

We can see that the sources of anger are many, all the way from reaction to a hostile act to a frank injustice. A person who reacts to anger by indulging in food is thus never at a loss for trigger mechanisms for compulsive eating.

Chapter Eight

Self-Deprecation

I have noted that anger and resentment are frequent triggers of compulsive overeating, and I indicated that we must find ways to overcome these. There is one type of anger that is particularly difficult, and that is anger at oneself. Some people find it easier to forgive others than to forgive themselves. While it is true that some people operate with double standards and are much more lenient in judging themselves than others, the opposite is also true, and we may be much harsher on ourselves than on others.

A person who has a positive self-image has much less difficulty coping with anger and its side effects. First, you have greater trust in yourself and less fear of losing control. Second, you are less likely to consider feelings of anger as being evil and sinful. Third, your ego is less sensitive, and you are less vulnerable to being provoked by inconsequential stimuli. Finally, you can accept guidance and other kindnesses with gratitude instead of being threatened by them. The culprit here as elsewhere is the bad fantasy self, because it is the erroneous self-perception that results in frequent recourse to the refrigerator to deal with ineffectively managed anger.

The inability to forgive oneself can result in a vicious cycle for the compulsive eater, because each failure to control the overeating generates self-deprecation. If that then triggers a binge, you are caught in a self-reinforcing cycle of: anger (from whatever source) → overeating → sense of failure → anger at oneself → overeating . . .

Dismissing our mistakes and failures as being of no consequence is irresponsible. Mature adults accept responsibility for their behavior. However, it is also wrong to allow ourselves to be so dragged down and consumed with self-incrimination that we are drained of all initiative and energy to act constructively. A healthy attitude is to acknowledge our mistake or failure for what it is, try to analyze why it happened, try to make the necessary corrections, and try to make another attempt at success. If we have offended or injured anyone, we should have the fortitude and courage to apologize and make amends wherever possible.

Human beings have many strengths but also many frailties. The aphorism, "Experience is a hard teacher but fools will learn no other way," is incorrect. Fools are those who do *not* learn from experience. It is the wise who learn from them, and there are not too many things in life that we learn the easy way. While discovering our mistakes may be unpleasant, we should look at them as learning experiences, and this attitude can eliminate much of the negativity associated with them.

Some people are able to do this without much difficulty. They take a failure in stride, learn from their mistakes, and go on with life. Others, however, get so bogged down that they are virtually paralyzed, or they expend inordinate effort on preventing the disaster of failure. Some of our actions have far-reaching consequences, but even then there is nothing to be achieved by hanging on to guilt.

All the world's religions have recognized human fallibility and have provided means whereby a person can expiate his or her guilt. Refusal to forgive oneself is akin to denying one's fallibility. It is ironic that self-deprecation and self-incrimination are actually a consequence of an attitude of omnipotence: "I should never have done wrong. I should be incapable of doing wrong. I should be perfect."

Inability to forgive ourselves can "eat away" at us, and we may try to "eat away" our distress, paradoxically causing more failure. If we can shed the attitude of omnipotence and recognize our vulnerability to error, we may diminish the need for recourse to food.

The attitude of omnipotence is apt to be a defense against feelings of impotence, unworth, and incompetence, all characteristic of the bad fantasy self. If we can accept ourselves with our inherent imperfections, we have no need for grandiose delusions of omnipotence. It might help if we realize that a baseball player who bats .300 makes millions of dollars a year, even though he gets a hit only three out of ten times; seven times he is out."

Cheryl is extremely self-critical. "I don't go to church anymore because I don't believe even God can love me," she said. I told Cheryl about a talk I heard at a support group for family members of recovering alcoholics. One woman, who had a child with Down syndrome said, "When I hold Chrissy in my arms and I know how much I love him even with all his imperfections, then I know how much God must love me, even with all my imperfec-

70

tions." Sure, we should always try to improve ourselves, but let us not be intolerant of ourselves.

Do we all make mistakes? Of course. We should not take decision making lightly, especially when our decisions are of major importance to ourselves or affect other people. All we can do is use the best information available to us, the best advice we can get, and then try to do the best we can with the utmost integrity. No one has prophetic foresight, and we have no way of knowing how things will eventually turn out. Of course, we see in hindsight many of the things that we could not foresee. A decision made with the best efforts possible is a morally good decision, even if the consequences are not good. It is absurd to feel guilty for failing to predict the future.

Guilt, like physical pain, can have an important function. The knowledge that we will feel guilty if we do something wrong often deters us from doing it. The guilt that we feel if we have done something wrong leads us to make amends. But when we sincerely regret our mistakes and resolve not to repeat them, and when we have done everything possible to make amends to whomever we did wrong, we should then let go of the guilt, because it serves no purpose. This nonproductive guilt may result in our being angry at ourselves, and resentment against oneself is frequently a cause of compulsive behavior.

The self-recrimination, "Why am I like this?" is indicative of a defeatist attitude, because it assumes a fact, "I am like this" or "I am a loser at this," and just asks why this is so. The premise is wrong. We should not resign ourselves to "I *am* like this" but rather "What I did was a mistake" and then set ourselves to avoid the same mistake. There is a subtle difference between thinking "Why *am* I like this?" and "Why did I *do* that?" but it is an important one. "Why am I like this?" is a negative attitude about myself, whereas "Why did I *do* this?" addresses what I *did*, not what I *am*. A positive attitude—"I am a good capable person, but I made a mistake"—is conducive to positive achievement.

It should be evident that how we think of ourselves determines whether we see a failure as an unpleasant incident that can serve as a learning experience, or as further evidence of our inadequacy. Someone who has a negative self-concept, whose self-image is the bad fantasy self, interprets a failure as further confirmation of inadequacy, whereas someone who has a positive self-concept looks at a mistake as an unpleasant occurrence and tries to focus on "What must I do to avoid repetition of it?"

Chapter Nine

Relationships

In articles or on television we generally find statements like "Food is equated with love" or "Food has become a substitute for relationships." There seems to be rather universal agreement about this. Let us see why this may be so.

In virtually every case of compulsive eating there is an element of isolation. The isolation may be almost complete, with the compulsive eater withdrawing into a cocoon, or it may be selective. The person may relate to others at work or socially but withdraw from intimacy.

It is easy to see why this happens. If you are a compulsive overeater, much of your time is not available for relationships, because you are preoccupied with either fighting off the compulsion or yielding to it. The time and energy that could be expended in meaningful relationships are drained off in dealing with the compulsion. For example, you may be spending more time than is necessary shopping for food, or watching TV shows on cooking, or collecting recipes, or just daydreaming about food. At weddings or other parties you may spend too much time at the buffet tables, and because you feel guilty about what you're eating, you take your plate and retreat to some corner where you can eat unnoticed. If you are not yielding to the compulsion to eat, you may be anxious, tense, grumpy, and frustrated, and your mood is not conducive to pleasant social interactions. If you attend a celebration while you are in the midst of an abstinence phase, you may be angry with yourself because you can't have fun like normal people. Either way, whether fighting or giving in, compulsive eating detracts from the ability to relate.

Needless to say, if you are overweight, or if you are self-conscious about weighing a bit more than you think you should, you may feel ashamed and embarrassed and wish to avoid being seen by others.

While the theme of the real you versus the fantasy self relates primarily to character and personality, every person also has a *physical* self-concept, which, like the personality self-concept can be true or false. As noted earlier, our self-perception is very real. We generally do not question our sensory perceptions. We conduct our daily lives on the assumption that what we see, hear, and feel are real and factual. By the same token, we assume that what we see and hear and feel are similarly experienced by everyone else who is exposed to the same stimuli.

It is no different in regard to the self-image. If you think of yourself as fat and unsightly, you conclude that everyone else sees you as fat and unsightly. This can even turn into a frank delusion. If you feel fat even though you are only six pounds above your desired weight, you may believe that everyone sees a grossly fat person, even though the truth is that they think that you are quite shapely. The self-image can be so far off base that you think you are obese even when your weight is ideal. In cases of anorexia, girls look at themselves in the mirror and count the protruding ribs while thinking themselves to be overweight and in need of losing a few more pounds!

Certainly in most social relationships, people couldn't care less what size dress you wear and are just as pleased to relate to you if you are forty pounds overweight or if you are Twiggy. Although that is the fact, that is not how you see it, and to you, your perception is reality. If you think you are grotesque, that is how you feel others think of you. Since no one wants to be thought of negatively, the person who is weight-conscious is likely to withdraw from contact with people.

Healthy relationships of any kind are based on a mutual exchange: Both parties give and receive. The exchange is not necessarily always equal, nor need it be for a healthy relationship. One partner may be giving somewhat more than the other, but not in the extreme. If either partner is all giver or all taker, the relationship is unstable, top-heavy, and usually fails. Of course, the relationship we have with food is primarily top-heavy. We only *take* from food and are not required to give anything in return. Food provides unconditional pleasure. The only reason this relationship can continue indefinitely is because the food cannot leave.

Compulsive eaters are almost invariably people of emotional extremes, and they tell you so. As one woman so aptly put it, "I love hard, I hate hard, I work hard, and I play hard." They are generally highly sensitive people and tend to overreact to stimuli.

Being oversensitive is not a blessing. I remember when we bought our first hi-fi phonograph. Our previous phonograph did not produce the best sound, but on the other hand, I didn't have to walk softly on my tiptoes to

75

prevent the needle from jumping off the groove as was the case with the new machine. The hi-fi was indeed much more sensitive, but it had to be treated with greater delicacy.

Most people react to stimuli with moderation. Of course, they are moved to intense emotion by things that should evoke an intense response. Compulsive eaters, by contrast, react with an intense emotional response to things that are relatively insignificant, and they are very easily hurt.

I have noted that compulsive eating may be an attempt to ease emotional discomfort. Just how much discomfort will people tolerate before they seek ways to relieve it? This is quite variable. Just as some people have a high threshold of physical pain and tolerate the dentist's drilling with hardly a grimace, others insist on having local anesthesia before the dentist dares touch them, because they cannot take any pain. The variability of tolerance of emotional discomfort is similar. Some people can take much distress in stride, while others can bear very little. People who can withstand emotional pain are less likely to turn to food for relief.

Mildred was a graduate student who was bulimic. I asked her whether she was aware of any specific things that triggered a binge. "Oh, yes," she said. "Someone just has to look at me the wrong way, and I go for the chocolates. If my boyfriend wasn't as demonstrative as I wanted, I gorge myself. But then I'm afraid he won't like me if I'm fat, so I throw up."

Emotional hypersensitivity and overreaction do not make for easygoing relationships. It is not easy to relate to a person who overreacts to an innocent comment with an angry outburst or a flood of tears. No one likes to be in a relationship where he or she is constantly guarding against saying something that will be taken personally. Furthermore, people whose sensitivity threshold causes them to be hurt very easily may try to avoid interacting with people. It is like someone with a severe sunburn who avoids entering a crowded elevator because even superficial contact hurts.

Add to this emotional hypersensitivity the preoccupation with one's self-image and the anticipation of derision, and it's easy to understand why compulsive eaters withdraw.

I mentioned that the relationship with food can continue indefinitely because the food does not have the option to leave. If you relate to another person the way you do to food, essentially "engulfing" the other person, he or she may indeed leave the relationship.

Compulsive eaters tend to become overdependent on people, and this can certainly place an intolerable stress on a relationship. People like to do things for others, but when the demand is constant, unyielding, or otherwise excessive, the burden may be too great to bear.

Yvonne was thirty-six, and lived with her mother. While she was efficient at her job, she was totally dependent on her mother at home. Her mother did all the housework, laundry, and shopping. The mother had to make Yvonne's doctor's and dentist's appointments, remind her when the car needed inspection, and keep track of all her papers for income tax preparation. Her mother complained that it was too much for her to look after Yvonne as if she were a child. Yvonne was overdependent, and her mother was actually encouraging her overdependence by doing everything for her. Her mother also made the rich pastries that contributed to Yvonne's overweight.

The other side of the coin is the compulsive eater who tries to control people by manipulating them. No one likes to be manipulated. In a healthy relationship there is an appropriate interdependence, with no one making inordinate demands on the other and no one trying to control the other person.

The emotional responses of compulsive eaters are somewhat similar to those of children. Whatever children want at a particular moment is all-important. They may cry bitterly over what appears to be trivial to an adult. Children are understandably dependent on their parents, but the dependency is tolerable because there is an end point in sight. The parents expect that children will eventually become self-sufficient. Children also manipulate parents, but this, too, is somewhat more tolerable because they usually grow out of it. Furthermore, parental love for children makes the challenges and stresses of raising them easier to bear.

The juvenile emotions of the compulsive eater may be caused by arrested development. An alcoholic woman who was to be discharged from the hospital led me to this insight. She said, "I began drinking at age fifteen, and as a result of my drinking my emotional development stopped at that point. I am now thirty-seven, and I have a sixteen-year-old daughter at home. It is frightening to think that I have to function as a mother to a young woman who is emotionally one year older than me."

Emotional maturation does not develop with chronological age but results from adjusting to life situations and mastering various challenges. There are some challenges appropriate to master at age ten, others at age fifteen, others at twenty, and so on. If instead of coping with age-appropriate challenges we escape from them, our emotional maturation is arrested. Regardless of what method of escape is used—alcohol, food, drugs, sex, or simply indolence—the chronologically mature adult may be fixated at a juvenile level emotionally, and this is what happens with many compulsive eaters.

I know firsthand how children, like adults, escape challenges that appear overwhelming. When I was ten, I was deathly afraid of a bully at school who used me as his punching bag. I told my mother, who came to school and shouted at him, but this did not change things. I was a good student and liked school but I didn't enjoy getting beat up.

One fall, at the beginning of fifth grade, I came down with hay fever, and the doctor prescribed a medication that knocked me out for twenty-four hours. My father, who was not a hypochondriac but panicked if any of us was sick, had two doctors examine me, and one doctor said he heard a heart murmur. That really frightened my father, although the heart murmur was not significant and has never caused me any difficulty. But I played it for all it was worth. I was sick, I had heart trouble, and I couldn't go to school. I managed to use that heart murmur to stay home from school for four months. A tutor came to the house, and I was safe from the bully. I had frequent heart examinations and enough fluoroscopy to kill a whole city with radiation.

After four months the cardiologist decided there was nothing wrong with me and I could go back to school. I reacted by throwing up. My parents then arranged for me to be transferred to another school. I had used illness as an escape and as a tool to manipulate my parents.

Looking back, I'm glad my parents had me transferred. Had I remained at the first school under constant threat of the bully, I might well have developed heart symptoms, and a single incident could have developed into a pattern. My hyperconcerned father was a sitting duck for becoming a codependent, and I could easily have become a cardiac cripple. It takes careful judgment to know when to cope with a challenge and when to extricate oneself from intolerable stress. This is one of life's toughest assignments.

If escaping becomes a pattern and we do not cope with age-appropriate behavior, we lose the raw material out of which emotional maturity is formed. If we discover escapist tendencies, we should be aware that we have some makeup work to do in emotional growth. Implementing the latest miracle diet is not going to help us achieve this growth, without which we cannot expect to have healthy relationships.

Chapter Ten

A Not-Too-Helpful Helper

Earlier I noted that compulsive eating is generally a result of a combination of factors, one of them being "environmental." Think of it this way: If you have a sapling palm tree, good soil, and fertilizer, and you plant the tree in a cool climate, it will not grow. The palm tree needs a hot climate in which to take root and grow. Much the same is true of compulsive eating; there are environmental factors that affect its emergence and persistence. Most important among these factors is the family. Family members do not cause compulsive eating any more than a hot climate produces a palm tree, but they can provide a "climate" in which compulsive eating can occur.

Contrary to the approach some psychotherapists take—looking for what initiated the problem—a much more effective approach is to help eliminate the factors that allow the problem to continue, the "oxygen" of the problem, as it were. We often find such "oxygen," or enabling factors, among the family that loves the compulsive eater and wants to help her. What they do not realize is that what they consider helpful is actually harmful.

There is a terminology regarding eating problems that should be clarified to avoid misconception. The compulsive eater is often described as "food dependent," and people in the environment of the compulsive eater are referred to as "codependents." "Dependent" and "codependent" are not pejorative terms and should not be misunderstood as such. There is healthy dependency and unhealthy dependency, and there is healthy and unhealthy codependency. No person is an island, and no one is totally self-sufficient. In some way or other every human being is dependent on other people, and the people upon whom we are dependent are "codependents." Obvious examples are a child who cannot provide for himself, or a person with an injury or an illness who must have the help of others.

These examples help define healthy versus unhealthy dependence and codependence. When the reality is that a person cannot care for his own needs, as a child or a sick person, then his dependency is healthy and the codependent caring for him is healthy. When a person can care for himself but instead wishes others to do it for him, that is unhealthy dependency, and adhering to his wishes is unhealthy codependency.

It should be obvious why this is so. Just as a muscle increases in strength when it is exercised and weakens when it is not used, so it is with many of our capabilities. If we do not use them, they "waste away," as it were, and if someone provides for us so that we do not need to exercise these capacities, we eventually become unable to provide for our own needs and become helpless.

Let me give you a personal example. I am essentially computer ignorant, but I found that a word processor would save me much time and effort in editing. I purchased a computer identical to that of my son who lived nearby, and instead of reading the instruction manual and learning how to operate the apparatus, I asked my son to show me how, which he dutifully did. When I encountered a problem, I called him for instructions, and if these did not resolve the problem, he would drop over and correct it. This arrangement worked well until he moved to another city, and I was left with a complex apparatus that I did not know how to use. I soon found myself under pressure to complete several articles rapidly approaching deadlines, and I had neither the time nor patience to consult the operating manual and begin learning from square one.

If my son had initially said, "Dad, there is a manual that comes with the computer. Study it and learn how to operate it yourself. If there is something you don't understand, call me," I would have developed at least basic computer skills, which would have been extremely beneficial to me. My mistake was asking for help with something I could have done myself, and my son's mistake was responding to an unhealthy dependency request.

We may ask for unnecessary help because we are too lazy to do for ourselves, or because we think we are incompetent. Those who respond to these requests either unwittingly encourage our indolence or confirm our feelings of inadequacy. Although the codependents mean to be helpful, they do not realize that the "help" is counterproductive.

The inability of codependents to see that their help is actually counterproductive may be due to their own needs to be helpers. Some children learn early in life that to win parental approval and to have a sense of worth they must be helpers, and as they mature they are not able to divest themselves of this orientation. This need to help can result in constructive expression if the person becomes a doctor, nurse, teacher, social worker, or other provider of human services. It can be constructively expressed as a parent or spouse who cares for the realistic needs of a child or spouse. However, if parents infantilize their grown-up children and keep them dependent, or if a spouse fosters unhealthy dependency, the emotional needs of the codependent to be a helper are detrimental to the dependent person.

The psychological needs of the codependent may be inordinately great, and hence she feels that without someone to care for she has little worth. This results in her virtual inability to allow the dependent to become self-reliant, because this would do away with her being needed.

In many cases of compulsive eating, we find more than one codependent. The behavior of codependents is sometimes more difficult to understand than that of the compulsive eater. Thus, the parent or spouse or children of the compulsive eater may try to help with the diet, eliminating foods they enjoy from the house, encouraging or even monitoring exercising, and sometimes expressing themselves as, "If you really loved me you would do it for me." Any failure in the weight-loss regime is not only distressing in itself but also causes the compulsive eater to feel guilty for disappointing the codependents and to feel that her behavior is an expression of "I don't love you enough to stay on my diet." The codependent feels sorry for the compulsive eater and at the same time is very angry with her. This results in a hodgepodge of conflicting feelings on everyone's part, including love, anger, frustration, expectation, and disappointment. The attempts to conceal the negative feelings only result in even greater confusion. The emotional climate of the dependent-codependent home is totally chaotic.

Emerging from an unhealthy dependent-codependent relationship is difficult, and is often met with resistance from both sides. Ideally, both dependent and codependent should avail themselves of counseling or the support of a self-help group.

Parents and spouses want their children or spouses to be happy, and they try to do things that will make them happy, or at the very least will relieve their distress. Just as compulsive eaters opt for the short-term goal of relieving discomfort by eating and lose sight of the long-term consequences, so codependents try to provide short-term relief and do not consider the long-term disadvantages. Parents and spouses are therefore prone to go along with the compulsive eaters' methods of feeling better for the present, by either giving tacit approval to their eating habits or even actually encouraging them, as by baking things the compulsive eater should be avoiding.

Parents take pleasure in helping, and their grown-up children may not wish to deprive their parents of the opportunity to be helpful. When this help is counterproductive, it precludes the child from developing strength and self-esteem, which are so crucial in overcoming compulsive eating. The dependent child feels she is bad if she does not allow her parents to cook for her, and she thinks she is being a dutiful child by visiting her parents every day.

I don't want to alienate children from their parents. Far from it. Parent-child relationships are precious and should be maintained, but they should not be smothering. Grown-up children should love their parents and share with them, but they should be independent. The compulsive eater often has tendencies to remain dependent because it is more comfortable, and eliminating unhealthy dependencies may be distressful to both the compulsive eater and the codependent parent or spouse. It is helpful for the compulsive eater to understand why codependents act the way they do, so that she can help restructure the relationship. In some cases, the compulsive eater places the responsibility for her recovery on the codependent. "You watch my diet. Wake me up early enough so that I can do my exercises. Come with me to Marcy's wedding and make sure I don't binge."

Overcoming compulsive eating is a challenge, and the triumph is feasible only if the compulsive eater sees and accepts that challenge as her own. This cannot occur as long as the codependent is trying to manage or control things for her.

A husband who loves his wife or a parent who loves his child frequently says, "I cannot sit idly by and watch her destroy herself." The fact is, however, that the codependent really has no choice. Whether the compulsive eater improves or deteriorates is not going to be affected by the codependent's behavior, except that to the degree the codependent tries to fix things, the compulsive eater will relax her own efforts.

The advice to the codependent has often been expressed as "detach with love." This does not mean detach oneself from the compulsive eater and not be concerned about what happens to her. Instead, detach oneself from the compulsive eater's *problem*, not from the person. Detaching from the problem is necessary because there is nothing you can do about it, and the sooner this is realized and accepted, the better off everyone will be. The compulsive eater should encourage such detachment.

There are several reasons why a codependent should

detach (from the problem, not from the person). Primarily, this puts the responsibility of recovery squarely where it belongs: with the person who needs to recover. But there are other reasons as well. As long as codependents are busy trying to fix someone else's problem, they do nothing about their own.

We all have areas in our lives that could bear improvement, but if we are preoccupied with someone else's problem, we do not attend adequately to our own. Furthermore, we may think that failure of the dependent person to improve is a reflection on ourselves. For example, the wife of an alcoholic thinks that people will attribute her husband's drinking to some shortcomings on her part: "If you were married to her, you'd drink too." Similarly, the family of a compulsive eater feels that her appearance is a reflection on them, and they then try to "help" the person, while the real motivation is to help themselves. When we do things ostensibly for the benefit of others but are in fact motivated by personal interest, we end up doing things that are actually disadvantageous to the other person.

Codependents allow people to determine how *they* feel. It is understandable that when someone you love is happy, that makes you feel good, and if he or she is sad, that makes you feel bad. That is only normal and should not be otherwise, but we should not be totally at the mercy of someone else's emotional state. The dependent person has a large enough task tackling her problem without the additional burden of concern that she is making others miserable. Detaching oneself from the problem of the dependent thus actually makes her task easier.

Although the compulsive eater must cope with the challenge of her recovery, she should realize that her mother or husband is also being challenged. It is not her prime task to deal with their problems, but statements like, "Mom, I will love you just as much even if you won't bake my favorite cake," or, "Honey, I appreciate the chocolates, but I know you love me and you don't have to prove it by bringing home candy," can't hurt.

It is not easy for codependents to detach. They feel that they are abandoning the dependent person. Reading about codependency may help, but there is really no substitute for counseling, either by a therapist or a support group. A better understanding of codependency can enable one to overcome the erroneous feelings and allow the dependent person the freedom to recover.

Chapter Eleven

Is It Really Someone Else's Fault?

Codependency isn't the only relationship pitfall to watch out for. Subscribing to the "blame game" can also prevent compulsive eaters from dealing with their problems, which might call for some changes in themselves that are uncomfortable and inconvenient. It is much easier to say, "I can't help being the way I am. It is my mother's fault" (somehow, mothers get the lion's share of the blame).

Since we spend the formative years of our lives with our parents, there is no question that they exert a major influence on our development, and I grant that they may even have been responsible for the emergence of some psychological disorders. But so what? Self-pity won't get you far in overcoming the problem, and if you have a compulsive eating disorder, self-pity can result in a whopper of a binge.

The overwhelming majority of parents are well intentioned and wish to do the best for their children. Bear in mind that our maximum wisdom comes at about age sixty-five, when we have learned much from the experiences of life, but that is not when we raise our children. Child rearing occurs when we are the least wise. With all our good intentions, we make mistakes.

There is no way to reverse or undo the past, and there is therefore little reason to dwell on it. Current relationships with parents may affect an eating disorder, since parents are often codependents. But even here the emphasis should not be on faulting the parents. Accept them for what they are, because they do love you, even if you don't agree with them. That is reason enough to forgive them for mistakes they have made. Make the necessary changes in *yourself* to relate to them in a manner that does not contribute to perpetuation of your eating disorder. Obviously, if parents seek help for themselves and are able to discontinue their codependent behavior, your job is that much easier, but you can't control what your parents do. *You* have to make the necessary changes *in yourself*. The same holds true for spouses, siblings, and friends.

I have placed great emphasis on self-awareness and self-esteem. There is nothing easier in the world than to blame one's low self-esteem on one's parents. "After all, they were the ones who spanked me, and shouted at me, and sent me to my room." What you are saying is, "I really would have thought much better of myself if not for the things my parents did to me." Okay. I agree. But even if you are what your parents made you, you don't have to stay that way. Confronting your problems and doing what is necessary to correct the distortion your parents caused you to have can generate a great deal of self-esteem and help you on your way to a healthy independence.

Chapter Twelve

Acting as If

Some of the behaviors that we see in the compulsive eater are not unique. They also are found in people who are not compulsive eaters. In those cases, these behaviors are often part of other maladaptive techniques to living in reality.

This is the punch line: *living in reality*. Have no doubt about it, reality is rough. Even if we set aside the disasters created by people—crime, abuse, wars—there is much in nature that is distressing—earthquakes, floods, fires, and the like. On a more individual scale, there are diseases, injuries, and serious setbacks like job loss. There is also much beauty in the world and much to enjoy, but that usually doesn't make up for the hardships.

Yet there is often not much option. In some cases we have the ability to take the sting out of reality, as when we escape from the torment of torrid heat by turning on the air conditioner. Very often, however, we are unable to alter circumstances to conform to our desires, and the only option is to adapt ourselves to the circumstances. This is well summed up in the Serenity Prayer: Accept the things that cannot be changed, and change the things that should be changed.

There is, however, another option, albeit a destructive one: neither accepting nor changing an unpleasant reality but trying to escape from it. This is, of course, what happens when you drown your sorrows in food. The unpleasant reality does not change, nor do you accept it.

It should be evident that the latter approach is self-destructive. Refusing to accept an unchangeable reality and refusing to adapt to it as best you can invariably makes the situation worse.

We must adapt in order to cope more effectively with reality. But the changes must be *real*. Fantasy and make-believe accomplish nothing. This is beautifully portrayed by James Thurber in "The Secret Life of Walter Mitty," where the milquetoast husband escapes his wife's domination by pretending he is a triumphant hero. This adaptation of a particular role is a perfect example of escape.

Making changes in ourselves is not too difficult if we are flexible, but if we have become set in our ways and have developed a rigid personality, making changes can be a major ordeal and may be met with much resistance. Furthermore, once we adopt a particular role, all our behavior tends to be influenced if not determined by that role. Some actors have said that while they are portraying people of great spirituality and saintliness, they are unable to do things that are incompatible with that identity. It is much the same with any of the roles we adopt. Behavior inconsistent to that role is avoided.

There are some roles that are adopted in response to

or in defense of our self-image. For instance, feelings of inadequacy or unworth may cause you to take on the role of a loser. Roles may be taken on in early childhood and continued throughout life, often reinforced by self-fulfilling prophecies. Thus, Charlie Brown sees himself as a loser, expects to lose, and goes on to lose.

Peanuts® by Charles M. Schulz. Reprinted by permission of United Feature Syndicate, Inc.

This pattern has its counterpart in compulsive eating.

A misguided compulsive eater may see herself as being the way she is because of the way everybody treats her. The husband, the children, other family members, her employer . . . everyone is at fault.

Being a victim may have its compensations, although these are pathological rewards. There is a kind of gratification in indulging in a pity party and feeling sorry for oneself.

Peanuts® by Charles M. Schulz. Reprinted by permission of United Feature Syndicate, Inc.

It is difficult for the "victim" to change an identity, and the difficulty may be compounded because her problem (obesity, bulimia) serves a function in the family dynamic. Anyone in the family who feels any kind of distress can attribute it to the "victim's" problem. "If Betty were only okay and happy, everything would be fine."

This is, of course, not true. All people must deal with

their own problems, but they may be able to divert the attention from their situation as long as they can see the compulsive eater as the one who is responsible for others' miseries and the one who must make the necessary changes in herself. Mind you, this is not thought out deliberately and consciously; it goes on at a subconscious level. If the compulsive eater recovered, the family members would be left without any explanation for their individual difficulties. To avoid being confronted with their own problems, something that would occur if the compulsive eater recovered, the family inadvertently undermines the recovery.

Think of the family as being analogous to the mobile suspended over an infant's crib. When the various pieces have achieved an equilibrium, they are stationary and at rest. If the position of a single piece is altered, all the other pieces now move to a new position to achieve a new equilibrium. This is true of the family system: When any one family member changes, even if it is for the better, the other members of the family must change accordingly. Since change of any kind is often uncomfortable, it is not surprising that family members are not thrilled with any change in any one of the family, even if it is for the better.

Some roles are not directly linked to compulsive eating but can have the same diverting effect. The role of the "caretaker" is often, but not exclusively, seen in homes where one or both parents are dysfunctional, and one of the children takes on a parental role. If a person, at whatever age, suffers from feelings of inferiority, being a caregiver may give her a sense of worth. While caregiving may be constructive and laudable, it can also have its drawbacks. First, it relieves the people who should really be providing care of their responsibilities. Second, it diverts the one who is using it as a compensatory mechanism from discovering that she is harboring a bad fantasy self, so she fails to take the necessary steps to correct the erroneous self-image. Finally, it is likely to become a rigid characteristic of one's personality, so that the person cannot function unless she is a caregiver.

There is a story about a person whose preacher delivered a moving sermon extolling the virtues of providing shelter for the homeless, feeding the hungry, caring for the sick, and burying the dead. Inspired to do good, the man found a homeless person and took him into his home. Since the hungry man had not had any real food for several days, the good samaritan gave him a lavish meal that he ate so rapidly that he fell sick. Now the man had the opportunity to care for the sick, which he did by giving him cathartics and other home remedies, overtreating him to the point where he died. He then arranged for his burial and felt himself to be extremely virtuous, having earned a heavenly reward by providing a home for the homeless, feeding the hungry, caring for the sick, and burying the dead.

The point of the story is that if you have a desperate need to vindicate yourself by being a caregiver, you may do whatever it takes to provide care for others. The classic example of this is parents who infantilize their grown-up children, doing everything for them and thereby making them dependent and thwarting their development of self-sufficiency. "Benevolent" caregivers can thus have a toxic effect on their "beneficiaries." In addition, they may become depressed in the event that their charges leave their care.

I had a patient who suffered from an intractable depression. When she was eight, her mother thrust the care of her younger siblings on her, and she rose to the occasion, assuming the maternal role, which she retained

97

throughout her life. She continued to care for everyone in her family in addition to her husband and two children. When the children married, she was left with the care of her husband, but when he died, she was aimless in life. She had ample means to travel and see the world and to participate in many senior citizen activities, but she could not enjoy anything that smacked of self-indulgence. The only adaptation she was comfortable with was to do for others, and when there were no recipients of her bounty, she felt totally worthless.

Another role is that of the "clown." This too is likely to begin early in life, where a child takes on the job of trying to entertain everyone in the family and keep them happy, perhaps to ease domestic strife. This may be cute for a youngster, but it easily develops into a pattern as an adult of being the stand-up comic, the joker, or the prankster. Such people may be pleasant company for a few moments, but they are intolerable over the long run. Being jolly has its virtues, but life is a serious business and cannot be dismissed as one big joke. These people are not able to have a lasting intimate relationship and are very lonely. While they may amuse others and appear to be eternally happy, the clown act conceals a very sad, needy, and frustrated person. Although this person provides mirth among company, the depression and lonely confines of the apartment are likely to trigger compulsive eating. Perhaps this is the origin of the concept of the "jolly fat person."

Another role is that of the "recluse." In childhood these people improve on the aphorism "children should be seen and not heard" by not allowing themselves to be seen either. They are exceptionally "good," never giving their parents any reason for grief. They are docile, quiet, and obedient, and keep to themselves. This, too, is a maladaptation to a negative self-concept, having the idea that they are unlikable and therefore better off keeping to themselves than being rejected by others. They are also often very passive and allow others to make decisions, because doing anything on their own initiative is apt to be wrong. They don't develop social skills, and the conviction that they are unlikable precludes intimate relationships. Recluses take nine-to-five jobs and return to lonely apartments with nothing to do evenings and weekends except eat.

Roles that are assumed, whether to compensate for an intolerable negative self-concept or to placate others, are false and are not expressions of the "real" self. The chronic frustration of the real self is likely to result in a smoldering depressed mood, with a persistent feeling that life is unfair. Along with the lack of self-expression, much ambition and creativity are thwarted. The talents of the recluse are buried under shyness and withdrawal, and those of the caregiver may never come to the fore because she is too busy expending energy to look after the needs of others. There is a pervasive feeling of discontent, with a person not having any ideas about just what it is that is frustrating her. The unexplained discontent may be projected onto any number of irrelevant factors and the distress anesthetized by food. Recovery requires (1) elimination of the anesthetic; (2) stripping away the "as if" role; and (3) bringing out and fulfilling the real self.

Chapter Thirteen

Perfectionism and Moralism

Compulsive eaters are often haunted by fear of failure. A person who has tried various diets and techniques to lose weight, only to have her sense of accomplishment dashed to smithereens when she regains, is understandably disappointed by failure. It is no fun to lose at anything, and it is particularly distressing when one has repeated failures.

Failure is never pleasant for anyone, yet it must be accepted as a fact of life: We win some and we lose some. A realistic attitude toward failure consists of taking it in stride and moving on to the next challenge. This attitude is difficult if not impossible for a person who thinks that she is inferior, because a failure confirms her feelings of inadequacy. For her failure is nothing less than devastating.

One way to deal with failure is to compensate for it by being extremely successful in other areas. Thus, someone who repeatedly fails in losing weight and maintaining weight reduction may try to compensate by proving herself to be extremely efficient in other areas. It is not uncommon for compulsive eaters to be very hard workers, diligently dedicated to their tasks and making great effort to achieve perfection in other things. We see an interesting pattern emerge in some compulsive eaters: excellent performance in work, countered with repeated failures in weight control.

The longer this pattern continues, the deeper it becomes ingrained in the compulsive eater's personality. She develops a comfortable equilibrium of success and failure, which persists as long as they are counterbalanced. Anything that upsets this equilibrium results in distress. If a compulsive eater runs into failure on the job, her reaction can be grossly out of proportion and result in severe depression. But strangely enough, too great a success can also upset the delicate balance. The compulsive eater may actually be driven to fail. [Simply on a statistical basis, the number of people who succeed in maintaining weight loss should be greater,] and one comes to the conclusion that some compulsive eaters are *trying to fail*.

As long as the success/failure equilibrium is maintained, the compulsive eater may be highly efficient. They are perfectionists who keep everything in the office well organized and at their fingertips.

It is also not unusual to find high standards of sexual moralism among compulsive eaters. Seeing oneself as unattractive is one way a woman can defend herself against fears of sexual involvement. Whether she avoids sexual involvement because of negative associations with sex, which may occur with someone who was molested in childhood, or because of a fear of being unable to control her sexual drives, her feelings of unattractiveness provide her with a sense of security. Having a shapely figure may

101

be threatening to her, because it deprives her of a defense against her fears of sexuality.

Perfectionists and moralists are preoccupied with doing things correctly and doing what is right. But what could possibly be wrong with that? It would appear that doing things correctly and doing what is right is an excellent guide to living.

True, but with some qualifications. For example, there is a correct way to drive an automobile, and a novice driver has to think consciously about every move. What lane should I be in? How should I position myself for a turn? At what point should I apply the brakes? What do I have to do to parallel park? Once you get the knack of it, all these things happen automatically. You get in the car and drive efficiently while listening to the radio or a tape, and you make all the necessary maneuvers in traffic *without thinking consciously about them.* Why? Because you have developed trust in your ability to drive, and you can operate on "automatic" rather than on "manual." Imagine what it would be like if every time you drove you had consciously to contemplate every move just as you did during your first week behind the wheel.

Perfectionists and moralists do not trust themselves. They have to think about everything they do because they lack confidence in their ability to operate on "automatic." They are afraid to let go. There is little doubt that this lack of trust in oneself is a consequence of an impoverished self-esteem, and many compulsive eaters have a profound lack of self-confidence. Going back into their history, we often find that they lacked self-confidence long before the eating problem developed. They developed perfectionistic traits and rigid personalities at an early stage in life. Once they get into compulsive eating, particularly when they begin to fail at their attempts to keep the pounds off, their self-confidence is further depressed, and the decreasing trust in oneself leads to more and more perfectionism and more rigid moralism.

With many compulsive eaters, this rigidity temporarily disappears when they binge, just as the alcoholic mellows with the first few drinks. But very soon the tranquilizing effects of food wear off, and with the realization that one has failed again, the rigidity comes back with a vengeance.

The rigidity that results from perfectionism poses a major obstacle to recovery. While changing eating habits is not easy, it pales in comparison to making changes in one's lifestyle, which is essentially the shedding of the fantasy self and reaching a true self-awareness. The latter is a fundamental and comprehensive change, and people with rigid personalities are most resistant to change.

Adjustment to change can be so stressful that people prefer to remain in an oppressive situation that is familiar to them rather than move into a more comfortable situation that is an unknown. For example, children who have fled from abusive parents often return home with the full knowledge that they will be severely beaten, because they can more easily tolerate familiar misery than the unknown.

Although discarding the fantasy self results in a much more positive self-image, there may be formidable resistance to making this change because it constitutes a move from the known to the unknown. Furthermore, as the compulsive eater undergoes change, codependents must undergo corresponding changes as they adjust to the new personality, and they too may be resistant to change. Persistence of traits in codependents makes it more difficult for the compulsive eater to change. This is why everyone, both the subject and the codependent, needs support in making the salutary changes, until a comfortable stability is eventually reached at a new level of functioning.

Chapter Fourteen

People Pleasing

One of the reactions to having poor self-esteem is "people pleasing." This is not unique to compulsive eaters; it is a mechanism frequently employed by people who wish to be liked but do not think people will like them. Convinced that they are unlikable, they try to "buy" affection by doing things for others. People pleasers cannot turn down a request and do whatever is requested of them even when this is at great self-sacrifice. They go out of their way to help others.

Is it wrong to do things for other people? Of course not. The world would be a much happier place if more people performed acts of kindness. But acts of kindness should be done for the right reason, that they are the decent and proper things to do, and one should extend oneself to help others. When done in this way, we enjoy doing favors for others and are left with a wholesome feeling.

But a people pleaser feels that if she refuses a request, she will alienate others. This person has a negative self-image and assumes that people do not like her. She does anything that is asked of her, whether she wants to or not, because she cannot risk the consequences of offending someone. Although she gives the appearance that she is happy to be of service, the truth is that she feels imposed on and resents whoever has requested a favor.

Feelings of resentment can trigger binges. Compulsive eaters handle resentments very poorly, and as with anger from any other source, they seek solace in food to assuage their discomfort.

The conviction that one is not likable is a result of a bad fantasy self. When relapse into overeating aggravates the preexisting negative self-image, people pleasers are caught in a destructive whirlpool. The intense negative feelings that result from their failure to lose weight aggravate their feelings of unlikability, which may lead to more people pleasing and so forth.

As mentioned, people pleasing can be found in anyone who has a negative self-image. However, the compulsive eater has a more complex problem. Over and above whatever feelings of unlikability she harbors, she now has additional insecurities because of her physical appearance.

Because they are so fearful of offending anyone, people pleasers are always apologizing for themselves. One young bulimic woman began crying during her interview and promptly apologized.

"Why are you apologizing?" I asked. "What were you doing that was wrong?"

"I should be able to control myself better," she said. "I shouldn't bawl like a baby."

I pointed out to her that it is appropriate to cry when one feels hurt, and since the material she was relating to me was painful to her, it was only proper that she cry. She then said, "I always apologize for everything."

I told the young woman that unnecessary apologizing is indicative of a low self-esteem, and that elevating her self-esteem is an important goal in recovery. I suggested that she begin taking some action right now—stop apologizing when it is not called for. I explained that corrective action can have a great impact on feelings, and that stopping apologizing unnecessarily would help dissipate her negative self-feelings.

As she left the office, there was a patient in the waiting room, to whom the young woman promptly said, "I'm sorry I took so much of the doctor's time and kept you waiting." We have spent our lives creating our habits. It is difficult to change them.

People pleasers tend to downplay themselves. Sometimes they express self-criticism because they anticipate others' criticism and try to beat them to the punch. Sometimes they are self-effacing to elicit a contradiction and reassurance from others. For example, "I'm sorry the centerpieces for the tables did not turn out right."

"What are you saying, Lorraine? They are absolutely gorgeous. Everybody is raving about them!" Although Lorraine may feel herself validated by this praise, it provides only a fleeting sense of self-worth, and the negative feelings soon recur.

People who can't say no to others find it equally difficult to say no to themselves. People pleasers who have little practice turning down requests by others have similar difficulty turning down their own emotional request to overeat. Recovery requires learning how to say no to others when this is appropriate, and also how to say no to oneself.

Chapter Fifteen

Denial

You may think that since you picked up this book you are well aware of the problems of compulsive eating and/or dieting and are sincerely searching for a way to overcome them. That may well be true, but it is not necessarily so.

One of the most fascinating phenomena in human psychology is *denial*. Psychologists use the term to refer to an *unconscious* process whereby a person is actually unaware of something factual. The person is not willfully distorting the truth but is rather unconsciously concealing the truth from herself.

An example of denial: A woman feels a tiny lump in her breast and quickly forgets that it is there. Automatically, without thinking, she avoids touching the area, which might cause her to face the truth. She is likely to switch television channels when there is mention of breast cancer, or to turn the page in a magazine when there is an article on the subject. It might seem as though she is consciously avoiding it, and occasionally this is so. However, she may actually be unaware of the lump and also unaware of her avoidance mechanisms. Why? Because the awareness of the lump and what it might mean is so threatening to her that her mind blocks it out. The knowledge that initially registered was quickly relegated to the unconscious portion of her mind, where it lies buried, and she unwittingly employs various defense mechanisms to keep it there.

Denial occurs when something is so threatening to us that we do not wish to acknowledge its existence. Some people who are grossly overweight think of themselves as pleasantly plump and add that this body build runs in the family and is normal. I have told some overweight people that they must bring their weight down for health reasons, and they have assured me that they are on a weight-loss regimen. They give me the same reassurance when I see them two months later, having lost no weight. Sometimes they add that they have been on an eight hundred-calorie diet for the past six months. These people are often convinced that they are telling the truth. Indeed, their three meals a day constitute no more than eight hundred calories; they are simply oblivious of their considerable snacking.

Some people will stick to their story under threat of perjury or even if they were told they would be shot if they lied. Why? Because they genuinely believe what they are saying. What about the quart of ice cream eaten last night and the candy wrappers strewn all over the car? The person in denial is as unaware of these as I am unaware of what is happening on the dark side of the moon.

Every once in a while there may be a breakthrough, like the sun shining through between a tiny break in the clouds on a heavily overcast day, but very quickly the awareness disappears. People will take the initial step to do something about a situation and then abandon the project. Many compulsive eaters have loads of books on the subject, cupboards full of diet foods, and even expensive exercise machines that were bought at a moment of awareness and then set aside as if there were no reason to use them.

Denial is a potent mechanism, working automatically to shield us from discomfort, just like a painful elbow automatically splints itself to avoid movement that can cause pain. If you try to move a person's rigid arm, she will resist you. "Please don't touch!" Exactly the same thing happens when you approach someone with a distressing reality. She keeps you at a distance. You may have avoided a friend who expressed sincere concern about your weight, or looked at some new fashions in a store window and remarked how unattractive they are. If these things have happened to you, it may have been your denial in operation, trying to protect you from feeling distressed.

Sometimes what is being denied tries to to push itself out of the unconscious into awareness. The psyche then reinforces the denial with any one of several psychological tricks to keep the material out of awareness. Foremost among these mechanisms is *rationalization*, which consists of giving logical-sounding excuses to cover up true reasons. Along with rationalization is often *projection*, which consists of diverting blame from the real source to another, in other words, projecting it onto something else. Some rationalizations are illogical or even absurd. For example, Joan's hypercritical mother-in-law is visiting for the holidays. She gets on Joan's case about the house-cleaning, how the children are being raised, even her appearance, and Joan finds herself bingeing on desserts to give her the strength to deal with her. Soon Joan is blaming her mother-in-law for her compulsive eating: "I wouldn't have eaten all those cookies if she weren't such a nag. It's all her fault."

Also common is the "I deserve it" rationalization. Julie has just finished a big project for her boss. For two weeks, she's been researching and writing reports without a moment to herself. As a reward for a job well done, she goes to McDonald's and orders two of everything . . . because she deserves it.

Other rationalizations are more encompassing. For example, "When I lose weight I'll get my life started again. I'll start dating, look for a job, and so on." This person is denying the real reason for not getting on with life. She is afraid to date, afraid of a relationship, afraid to apply for a job because she will be rejected or afraid to accept the job because of fear of failure. The obesity is an excuse, a rationalization, which allows the person to think, "I'm really not afraid of relationships and I'm not afraid to look for a job. It's just that the way I look now, I'm not presentable, but as soon as I get myself into decent shape, I will do all these things." It should be clear why attempts at losing weight fail. The obesity serves too important a purpose in the person's emotional economy.

Let me give you an example of how this works. Bert was treated for compulsive eating. A year after treatment, still eighty pounds overweight, he stated that he was unable to get on with his life. He couldn't hold a job and couldn't settle down in school. Bert said this was all due to a broken engagement and to his inability to get over being rejected by his fiancée several years earlier. We had several therapy sessions during which we discussed the relationship and his difficulty in adjusting to its termination, but Bert showed no change in his attitude.

The night after one session, I dreamed of an incident in my childhood. I was enchanted by rowboating, and the

111

thrill of my life was being allowed to take the oars and row. But of course I was never allowed to be in a boat alone. I would go down to the pier, and while the boat was securely tethered, I would row to my heart's content without any danger whatsoever. If the tether became loose, rowing would have been very dangerous, because I would be out in the middle of the lake, not knowing how to swim.

I awoke with a vivid recollection of the dream, and I realized what it meant, because this is precisely what Bert had been doing. Bert's real problem was that he was afraid of life, afraid of the responsibility of a job, afraid of doing poorly in school, afraid of being rejected in a romance. Because he did not want to recognize these fears, he rationalized and projected that the problem was his inability to get over the breakup of his romance. Bert had defensively "tethered himself to the pier." The rejection appeared to be a valid explanation and served the purpose of excusing him from trying. All therapeutic efforts at resolving the rejection were futile because *that was not his problem. The rejection was his solution.*

Being overweight may sometimes serve a purpose, so it cannot be easily let go of. The person who thinks her life can begin after she gets thin is likely to be much like Bert, afraid to let life begin, but inasmuch as it is humiliating to admit this to oneself, the unconscious mind exercises its ingenuity and says, "Look, you can't do all those things when you're fat. No one is going to fall head over heels in love with a fat person, and no one is anxious to hire a fat person. First get rid of the weight."

We can now see why there is resistance to losing weight, and we can understand at least one of the reasons why, if the weight is lost, it is so often regained. Maintaining the weight loss deprives a person of the needed excuse for not taking on other challenges of life. The anx-

112

iety thus provoked may *compel* (here is that compulsion again!) one to get the weight back, to tie the boat to the pier again in order to assure safety.

Why does a person have all these fears? It should be apparent that someone who is self-confident is unlikely to anticipate and have intense fear of failure and rejection. First, she has no reason to expect that these will occur, and second, if they should occur, it is not the end of the world.

A person with good self-esteem can take setbacks in stride. If you know your real self, there is more self-confidence and self-esteem. It is the fantasy self—the artifact put together by the opinion of everyone else that has no secure foundation—that is so fragile that every challenge appears formidable. Instead of dealing with the fear of challenges, you focus on something that seems more easily manageable: food.

Chapter Sixteen

Chemical Dependency

Dependency on mind-altering substances, whether alcohol or chemicals, is very common. There are some people who can drink safely, who do not drink excessively, and whose emotional status is not significantly affected by alcohol. There are some people who can take a tranquilizer, a sleeping pill, or a painkiller and not develop any dependency on these. There are others who are adversely affected by any mood-altering chemical. We do not yet fully understand why some people react differently to chemicals. There is reason to suspect a genetic vulnerability, and children of a parent who had an addictive condition are at a higher risk of becoming chemically dependent.

One of the high-risk populations for dependency are compulsive eaters, for whom exposure to a mood-altering chemical carries a greater risk of developing dependency. People who turn to food for relief of distressing feelings—anxiety, depression, self-consciousness—may also turn to medications for relief, and a well-intentioned physician may prescribe a tranquilizer to help ease that distress. This is fraught with danger of dependency. There are a number of diet pills that have mood-altering properties, and these too may cause dependence.

The compulsive eater may experience anxiety that is unrelated to the eating disorder, or may develop anxiety as a result of the repeated frustrations and failures of adhering to a weight-loss regimen. She may feel that if she were only a bit less tense, maintaining the diet would be easier, and she may obtain a prescription from her physician for a tranquilizer.

Most medical schools do not provide adequate teaching on addiction, and some physicians still do not realize that the tranquilizers that are promoted as a boon to save humanity from the devastation of tension have a potential for addiction. A physician may see nothing wrong with helping someone who is fighting a battle to lose weight by prescribing one of the benzodiazepine drugs (Valium, Xanax, Ativan). These medications do relieve anxiety and tension for a few hours, and in order to remain free of distressing feelings, it may be necessary to use three or four doses daily.

Use of most tranquilizers results in the phenomenon of tolerance, that is, after a period of time, as little as a few weeks, the body becomes immune to the effect of the drug, and the anxiety returns. The person who has relied on medication for relief often increases the dose, which is effective until the body becomes immune to the new dose, leading to a further increase. If the physician is reluctant to increase the amount of medicine prescribed, the patient may go to several different doctors and get a prescription from each. Some people find a pharmacist who gives them all the medications they want for a price, and some people skillfully alter the doctor's prescription for a greater amount.

Eventually the increased dose of the tranquilizer is likely to cause confusion, memory lapse, mood swings, and incoordination, or it may cloud one's thoughts and delay reflex responses. Functioning on the job or at home becomes impaired, and automobile accidents occur. The person may realize that she is using too much medication, but any attempt to reduce the dose results in very severe withdrawal symptoms, including panic attacks, insomnia, tremors, and even convulsive seizures, essentially forcing the person to increase the dose again. *It may be more difficult to withdraw from addiction to tranquilizers than from heroin or cocaine.*

Because of the addiction potential, tranquilizers should be used with great caution and usually only briefly. Maintaining weight loss takes a lifetime. As compulsive eaters have a higher than average potential to become addicted to mood-altering chemicals, they therefore should avoid tranquilizers. If you have become dependent on these drugs, consult a specialist on addiction regarding the safest way to taper off.

Chapter Seventeen

Bulimia

Like many other mental health professionals, I had no awareness of the existence of this condition when I became a psychiatrist. My medical and psychiatric training were in the 50s and 60s, and the diagnosis of bulimia did not appear in the psychiatric nomenclature until 1980.

In 1977, a young woman was admitted to the psychiatric hospital for treatment of depression. She was a third-year medical student who had excelled in the first two years but was doing very poorly this year due to repeated hospitalizations for symptoms that baffled the physicians at the University Medical Center. Periodically she had severe swelling of her ankles and abdominal bloating, together with profound weakness and even confusion. She underwent the most rigorous medical workups. The only findings were imbalances of the minerals in her blood, but no one could explain why this was happening. It was suspected that she had a "silent" malignancy somewhere, or perhaps some disease such as lupus, or some rare viral infection, but in spite of every known laboratory test and consultation with leading specialists, nothing could be found. She became progressively depressed because of her inability to keep up with the course work and was hospitalized psychiatrically following a suicide attempt.

After several days in the hospital she confided to me that she had this strange practice of bingeing on food, then taking large amounts of laxatives—perhaps thirty to forty tablets daily—and several diuretics to produce diarrhea and fluid loss in order to bring her weight down. She was terribly ashamed of what she was doing, and said that she knew she must be "crazy" for doing this, but she couldn't stop herself. She told me that she couldn't afford the laxatives and was stealing them from the pharmacy.

This young woman was very bright and in every other way appeared perfectly normal. She could not explain her behavior, except to say that she was terrified of being fat. Although she was at the ideal weight for her height, she considered herself much too fat. She described how desperately she had tried to stop gorging herself with food and then purging herself with laxatives, and how she often cried because of her inability to stop. Although she knew full well that her symptoms were due to her excessive purging with laxatives and diuretics, she allowed herself to be put through expensive and risky tests during her repeated hospitalizations because there was no way she could tell her doctors what she was doing. "I knew they would think I was crazy and they would put me away, which is where I ended up anyway." She was convinced that she was the only person in the world who had such bizarre behavior, and she was terribly ashamed of it.

In the years that followed, reports of similar cases began appearing in medical literature, and the condition was finally given a name and placed in the psychiatric nomenclature: bulimia.

Naming the condition was an important step forward, because it began to draw people's attention to the condition, but a full understanding continues to elude us even to this day. There has certainly been a great deal of progress in describing the condition with some of its variations, and there are some effective treatments. There are also some theories that try to explain the condition, but none has been firmly established.

What we do know about bulimia is that it is primarily a gender-related condition, occurring mostly in girls and women. Its onset is usually in mid- to late adolescence, and on the average, six years elapse before the woman seeks help.

The one feature that is always present in bulimia is an obsessive preoccupation with weight, essentially an intense desire to be thin, together with a conviction that one is too fat. This conviction persists in spite of the fact that the woman may be at her ideal weight or even underweight. In all cases there is binge eating, although there may be great variations in what constitutes a binge, together with some mechanism whereby the woman tries to undo the effects of the binge by inducing vomiting, purging with laxatives and/or diuretics, fasting, or exercising.

The bulimic woman typically has a profound feeling of shame and/or guilt associated with her behavior. She goes to extremes to keep her family and friends from discovering her behavior, and the need to conceal it generally results in withdrawal and isolation. The bingeing invariably goes on in privacy, which may curtail socializing. She may not be able to eat with friends because of her self-consciousness about her eating habits. The fear of exposure causes her to lie, and it is not unusual for a woman to steal food if she cannot afford it.

The woman's life is completely taken over by the various aspects of this condition. Much of the day is spent thinking about food, about what to eat and how much she should not eat, and planning a diet. She must think of how she is going to explain to her parents or husband why she is not eating or why she spends so much time in the bathroom, or why the food bills are inordinately large. Communication is impaired because of her defensiveness and the overriding need to prevent anyone from suspecting the truth. The woman may be convinced that if her husband were to discover her "craziness" he would surely divorce her.

Some women thrive on being pregnant, because it is widely accepted that pregnant women have very strange eating habits, and she can attribute everything to the pregnancy. One woman told me that she conceived every year for five consecutive years, gaining more than twenty pounds each pregnancy, eventually to reach a weight of 260 pounds. It was a relief to her to be able to binge without having to purge, and everyone wrote off her weight gain to the effects of the pregnancies.

Bulimics tend to binge most often on snack or dessert type foods, like ice cream, pastries, and soft drinks. There may be some variation in frequency, but usually bingeing becomes a daily affair, except for those women who fast for several days in order to lose weight.

The woman may get herself to work, where she is likely to turn in an excellent performance. Many bulimic women are perfectionists and are extremely effective at their jobs. There is a stark contrast between their careful control of everything on the job and the total absence of control in their personal life. Many bulimics are overachievers and do extremely well academically.

I believe the role of self-esteem in the genesis of bulimia is extremely important. Western culture idealizes thinness and idolizes shapely women, and there is thus an association between fat and ugly. There is a psychological mechanism of "concretization," wherein a person objectifies and translates a feeling about oneself into a concrete representation of that feeling.

For example, a severely depressed woman was admitted to the psychiatric hospital after having attempted suicide. The reason she gave for her suicide attempt was that her parents refused to provide her with colored contact lenses. The lenses were to change the color of her eyes so that she would not be ugly.

This young woman was, in fact, quite attractive. I learned that a year earlier she had undergone cosmetic surgery to make her nose smaller. I asked the family to bring photographs of this young woman prior to the surgery, and as I suspected, the photographs did not reveal anything unattractive about her original nose.

I asked the family why they had allowed their daughter to undergo an unnecessary surgical procedure. They answered, "Doctor, if you had been in our shoes, you would have done the same thing. All we heard from morning to night was how homely she was because of her nose, and that no boy would ever be interested in her. She carried on for hours at a time, often crying bitterly, stating that if we loved her we would come up with the money for the operation.

"We finally took her to a plastic surgeon, who refused to operate because he saw nothing wrong with her nose. We consulted three more plastic surgeons, all of whom turned her down on the same grounds. Finally she found a money-hungry doctor who agreed to do the surgery for a huge fee paid in advance."

She was pleased with her surgery, and for several months there was peace and quiet in the house. She was told that it would take several months for the swelling of the tissues to recede, but after that she was sure would be attractive.

After several months passed, she started with the eyes. She insisted they were the wrong color, and that is why she was unattractive. It was a replay of her concern with her nose. When her parents refused to buy her colored contact lenses, she cut her wrists.

This young woman felt she was ugly *as a person*, and she projected this feeling onto her body, as if to say, "It is not me as a *person* who is ugly, but it is my *body* that is ugly, and my body can be changed." Any change in her body, as with the cosmetic surgery, would simply shift the focus to another part of her body.

This is what essentially happens with bulimia. The objective fact, to which any observer can attest, is that these women are not fat. They are at their ideal weight or less, but their *image* of their bodies is fat and ugly. The *body image of a bulimic is a delusion*. As is well known to anyone who has tried to divert a person from delusional thinking, no amount of arguing or rational discussion will change her mind. Similarly, bulimics simply do not accept any assurance that they are not fat. They know for a fact that they are too fat, and they must become thin. When they become thin enough, they will get their self-esteem back, but not until then. The delusion of body image and the conviction that she is fat may explain the drastic measures the bulimic takes to lose weight.

There is no satisfactory explanation for the bingeing.

122

Bulimics report that bingeing relieves their anxiety and stress or various other unpleasant feelings, whereas "normal" eating does nothing for them. The reason for their recourse to food may be no different from that of nonbulimic compulsive eaters, except that it is much more dramatic. Huge amounts of food can be ingested within a short period of time. The loss of control in eating has been compared to the drinking of some alcoholics, who cannot stop once they have taken the first drink. Indeed, some of the similarities between bulimia and alcoholism have led some experts to consider it an addictive-type disorder.

Low self-esteem is found in all bulimics, without exception. Careful questioning reveals that most of these women had low self-esteem preceding the onset of the bulimia. Of course, the bingeing-purging with the repeated failures to control it, the social isolation, and the associated guilt and shame greatly intensify the depressed self-esteem. Correction of the self-esteem, however this is brought about, is crucial to treatment and may be the single most important factor in overcoming the bulimia and maintaining the recovery. I have already noted that the depressed self-esteem is the result of a bad fantasy self, hence the correction of a self-image and the attainment of a valid self-awareness is most important in recovery from bulimia.

Chapter Eighteen

Depression

There have been recent reports of some people being successfully treated for compulsive eating with antidepressant medication. I commented earlier that attempting to achieve weight control by means of medication usually results in short-term success and long-term failure, and may also present a risk of addiction. Is there any validity to the use of antidepressant medication in eating disorders?

There are some cases where an antidepressant is helpful, but they represent a small minority of compulsive eaters. In fact, one of the problems posed by prescribing antidepressant medication for depressive illnesses is that it may cause these patients to *gain* weight, and they then develop weight problems even though they never had any previously.

Most people who suffer from what is generally called "clinical depression" lose their appetites and lose weight.

When the antidepressant medication restores their appetite, they regain the lost weight. The logical question therefore is: If antidepressant medication *increases* appetite, how can it be used to *decrease* the craving for food?

The answer is that antidepressant medication does not primarily increase appetite. What it does is treat the depressive illness. If loss of appetite is one of the symptoms of the depressive illness, the desire for food returns with successful treatment. It can happen, however, that an occasional depressed person has an *increased* food intake with depression, although this is more common with bulimia than with other compulsive eating. In such cases, successful treatment of the depression decreases the appetite.

We must understand, however, just what kind of depression is being treated in such cases. People whose depression is a reaction to some adverse happening in their lives, such as death of a relative, loss of a job, or financial reversal, are generally not "clinically depressed." Although they feel sad, it is a normal—and temporary—feeling given the circumstances, and normal feelings do not respond to medication. "Clinical depression" is not primarily a reaction to adverse circumstances, or if it does follow such happenings, it is out of proportion to the unpleasant incident. It also is long-term. Clinical depression is due to a disturbance in the level of neurotransmitters, certain chemicals that are involved in the transmission of messages from one nerve cell to another in the brain. This disturbance can give rise to a wide range of symptoms, of which appetite disorder is one. If the symptom happens to be overeating, as occasionally occurs in bulimia, then the antidepressant may indeed help.

It is certainly not uncommon for people who feel annoyed or dejected to raid the refrigerator. This kind of "depression" is not a "clinical depression" where there is an imbalance in the body chemistry, but the depression born of frustration, as when someone feels rejected, disappointed, or slighted.

Peanuts® by Charles M. Schulz. Reprinted by permission of United Feature Syndicate, Inc.

Eating your way out of frustration simply does not work, although you may delude yourself that you do feel better.

126

Peanuts® by Charles M. Schulz. Reprinted by permission of United Feature Syndicate, Inc.

Snoopy is happy that he has "forgotten" his girlfriend, but has he really forgotten her? If he *knows* that he has forgotten something, he is actually remembering it. To think that he has eaten his way out of a painful memory is simply self-deceptive.

The sad mood in cases of frustration may not be different from the mood of clinical depression, but the two conditions are in fact very different. When we eat in reaction to disappointment, there is no chemical imbalance in the body, and antidepressant medication therefore is not effective.

At the risk of being repetitive, I must point out that whereas the frustration that is felt on being disappointed, rejected, or slighted is normal, such feelings are understandably aggravated in people who suffer from . . . you guessed it, low self-esteem, which is invariably the result of a distorted self-concept or a fantasy self.

127

Since many compulsive eaters are always on the lookout for quick-fix solutions, they are likely to say, "True, compulsive eating as a result of clinical depression occurs only in a minority of cases, but I am one of that minority. I don't need to make any major character or lifestyle changes. All I need is a prescription for antidepressant medication and my compulsive eating problem will be solved."

Before concluding that you are the one-in-a-thousand exception to the rule, have yourself evaluated by a competent specialist to determine if you indeed have a clinical depression. In the event no one can tell for certain, and you are prescribed the medication, you should know within three to four weeks whether you had a clinical depression, because that is how long it usually takes for the medication to work. If you feel no different after four weeks and are still hungry, forget the antidepressant and begin to deal with the real problem, getting to know yourself, your real self.

Resorting to food as a reaction to disappointment is one of the major pitfalls in compulsive eating, because it sets up a self-reinforcing, self-perpetuating vicious cycle.

The initial solution to this problem is to have more things to feel good about. Any good feeling as a result of taking a drink, a drug, or food is at best transitory, and it is invariably followed by a letdown. If you have done something to advance yourself, such as increasing your knowledge in any way, improving your spirituality, or helping another person or some worthwhile cause, you get a good feeling that lasts much longer than that of a glazed doughnut. Such self-enhancing deeds, together with the other techniques I will describe for getting positive self-esteem, can eliminate this particular vicious cycle of compulsive eating.

Part Three

Getting Over Overeating

Chapter Nineteen

Eliminating the
Negative Chain Reaction

If you are operating with a bad fantasy self, you are highly vulnerable to a negative chain reaction. Any negative feeling—guilt, envy, anger—can set in motion a chain reaction that drives you to eat, just as it drives an alcoholic to drink. If you get rid of the bad fantasy self, the same stimuli that would have driven you to eat will be only minor irritants rather than triggers to overeating.

But getting rid of the bad fantasy self takes time. If you are now, say thirty-one, you have probably been looking at yourself negatively for about twenty-five years. It is unrealistic to expect that you can overcome that attitude in just a few weeks or months.

We have to begin somewhere, so let's begin with a positive statement about yourself. "I am a great person." You may say, "I don't believe that, so how can I say it? How is my saying that going to help?" My answer is that you really are a great person. Take my word for it.

"But you don't even know me. How can you say that

about me? Furthermore, if you knew what I do, you would never say that."

Prior to developing an interest in compulsive overeating, I worked with alcoholics and drug addicts, and in my career I have seen more than forty thousand of these cases. All of these people had poor self-concepts, ranging from moderate to extreme, and each one could give abundant reasons to substantiate his or her self-concept.

I watched many of these people get sober. I watched them undergo changes that border on the miraculous. I saw them discover the beauty and strength in themselves that they never thought existed. When I told them at the beginning of their recovery to give themselves positive self-affirmations, they all said, without exception, "I don't believe that about myself." I said, "Okay, fake it until you make it. Just look at where the self-deprecation has gotten you. Try my way for a change."

This is why I suggest that you begin by saying, "I like myself the way I am." You may say, "That is absurd. I'm thirty pounds overweight. I *hate* the way I am."

Just look at the woman who is only six pounds over her ideal weight and who thinks of herself as being grotesque, although you may wish you had her shape. Bulimics think of themselves as obese when they are at their ideal weight, and anorexics who look like inmates of a concentration camp think that they must lose a few more pounds to be attractive. Whether or not you like yourself with your present weight is thoroughly subjective. I assure you that other people like you the way you are.

"But," you may say, "*I* don't like myself the way I am. That's why I want to lose weight." Liking yourself the way you are still allows you to want to be better. There is no limit to improving yourself. For example, your car may run well and serve your transportation needs, yet you want a better car, and when you get a better car, you still want to upgrade to a more luxurious model. So liking yourself the way you are does not preclude your wanting to get better yet.

Eliminate negative statements. "I can't allow myself to eat [whatever]" is a negative thought, and the unconscious associates this with punishment. "I am going to make myself healthier and better" is a positive statement, a kind of reward. When you begin to have real rewards, you won't need to reward yourself with a fudge sundae.

Attitudinal changes do not come easily, but if what you want is the easy way, you're reading the wrong book. The easy way is one of the "miracle diets" or gimmicks that melt away excess weight as quickly as butter in a microwave oven—and of course, put it right back on. Attitudinal change is gradual and takes effort, and not only are the results long-term, but there are many other favorable changes in addition to weight loss.

Allow yourself exposure to be asked for a date, and accept it. Go out with friends for lunch. If you are considering a new job or think you have a raise coming, don't delay it until you lose weight.

You may be saying, "I'll never be able to lose weight. I'll never be able to enjoy eating. I'll never be able to wear my beautiful clothes. I hate the way I look." All of these negative statements are taboo.

The "one day at a time" approach that has resulted in recovery from alcoholism for people who drank copiously and destructively for thirty or more years will work for you too. Eliminate the word "never" from your vocabulary. Focus on today. It may seem trite to say that you can do nothing about the past and that the future isn't here yet, but it's true nevertheless. All you can do is to try to live healthfully today and do the best you can today. Inasmuch as there is nothing that you can do today about tomorrow's eating, it is futile even to think about it. Today's eating is all you can manage today, so stop wasting your effort on what you cannot do anything about, and you'll find you have the energy to do much about what you can do, which is today's eating.

Stable changes come about slowly. Upward progress is periodically interrupted with episodes of regression. This is normal, and a slip is not a devastating failure.

One winter day I walked to the post office to mail an important letter, and because the sidewalks were icy, I was careful how I walked. When I was halfway to the post office, in spite of my caution, I slipped on a hidden patch of ice. Although I broke no bones, I did get bruised, but I obviously was not going to remain lying where I had fallen. I got up and walked farther, this time exerting even more caution to avoid icy patches.

Although I had slipped and fallen, I had nevertheless progressed halfway to my destination. It would be grossly wrong to say that because I fell I was back home and had to start all over again. The slip did not erase the progress I had made.

This is how you must consider a slip in your approach to weight loss. It does not erase the progress you have made, and it can alert you to be a bit more cautious as you go on.

Chapter Twenty

Coping with Stress

Unless you were born with a significant handicap, you were endowed with all that you need to cope adequately with the normal stresses and challenges in life. Some of the stresses of life can be very trying and painful: illness, death of a loved one, financial reversals, broken romances, job loss. Yet we do have the capacities to cope with these. The problem is that if you have a bad fantasy self, you may lack the self-confidence to cope, and if you allow this attitude to prevail and to prevent you from coping, the challenge will get worse and you will have made a self-fulfilling prophecy.

Perceiving a challenge as being overwhelming sets into motion a defeatist attitude. One of the best ways to prevent this from happening is to find someone who is willing to listen and describe the problem to him or her. In my many years of psychiatric practice, I have seen countless people arrive at the solution to their problem in the process of presenting the problem to me. I will not deny that I contributed something, not necessarily in the way of advice but rather in helping them see the problem more clearly, so that they could find their solution. If you can find a person who listens to you, preferably someone who can help you clarify the problem, you will very likely discover within yourself the solution to the problem.

What about problems that really do not have a solution? Their solution is to accept the reality that is unchangeable and adapt to it as best possible. Escaping from difficult situations, whether by eating or drinking or drugging or in any other way, is always counterproductive.

But what if you just can't find anyone to whom you can relate your particular stressful situation? Then take a pen and paper and *write your problem*. It is surprising how in the process of transmitting your thoughts to paper they become clearer, and you may just discover a solution that you had overlooked. The writing does not have to be done in one sitting. On the contrary, it is better if you do it piecemeal.

Begin with the problem as you see it. Then stop and think: If the particular problem were out of the way, would everything really be okay, or would there still be things bothering you? If so, what are they? Do you see any connection between them and what you thought was your main problem?

If you don't see anything other than the first problem, leave the letter alone for a while and come back to it the next day. You might now feel differently. What about these other problems? Can you find any solutions for them? Is there someone whose advice you can ask about any of these?

The writing may turn out something like a diary. For example:

Monday, June 18th

My problem is that I'm overweight. No, I'm fat and I'm ugly. The kids want me to take them to the pool, and their friends will be there with their mothers. I wouldn't be seen dead in a bathing suit. I need to lose 40 pounds and I can't lose an ounce. That's my problem.

Tuesday, June 19th

I took the kids to the pool, but I wasn't going to take my robe off. Several other women were there, and they were fatter than me, and they were in the pool and seemed to be enjoying it. Why am I more self-conscious than they are?

Maybe I'm too self-conscious. I was self-conscious even before I was overweight. I don't like to be around people, especially strangers. I hate when Jim asks me to go with him to business parties. Everybody's talking, and I don't know what to say. I feel stupid.

Wednesday, June 20th

I told Jim that the reason I don't want to go to his office parties is that I feel out of place. He said that was nonsense. The conversation is not about things that I don't know anything about, but just ordinary conversation and that I know as much about things as everyone else does.

I think I'm still too fat, but I just can't seem to lose weight even if I'm on a diet.

I'm on a diet now, but when I get hungry, I nibble on whatever is around. Whom am I fooling? I'm not really on a diet at all.

Thursday, June 21st

If I go on a diet, I should really keep it. But I don't. I really have never been happy except for when I lost 20 pounds. I felt great. Why didn't I keep it up? I was so proud of getting into clothes I hadn't worn for a few years. Why didn't I stay happy if I was happy? Maybe because all kinds of things aggravate me and I eat to get relaxed. Maybe I need to find other ways of relaxing so I won't have to eat.

Friday, June 29th

I haven't written anything for a week. I think this is silly. Writing isn't going to help me. I called for an appointment at a weight-control clinic.

Saturday, July 7th

I was at the clinic yesterday. I paid $180 for the first visit and I'm to go back on Friday. But what if I lose weight and gain it all back like before? How come I was self-conscious before I was over-weight?

I met a woman there who was fatter than me. She had her stomach stapled six years ago and she lost 120 pounds, but has alrealy gained 80 pounds back. Maybe I should work on my self-consciousness before I spend more money on the clinic.

There's nothing wrong with continuing this writing for weeks. The weight problem did not come overnight, and it does not have to be resolved quickly. If you try to be honest with yourself and write your thoughts as they occur, you may discover things that you have to work on, which may well be the fuel that keeps the weight problem going. After a few weeks, read what you have written, underline all the points except for the diet parts, and begin to consider what you can do about these other problems.

Some people call from out of town requesting appointments. I suggest to them first to put their problem in writing to me. Sometimes I receive lengthy letters, but other times they call back to tell me that after having written out their problem, they began to see a way out on their own.

It is not my intention to deprive my psychiatric or psychologic colleagues of clients, but before running off to a therapist, do this simple paper-and-pen exercise. You may *think* you know exactly what you are feeling and why, but it may all appear different once you put it in writing. Don't hold back on any feelings. It is perfectly safe to be frank, honest, and revealing, because after all, you don't have to show your essay to anyone.

I recall a young woman who was about to do a take-off on her parents for the way they were treating her. I sensed what was coming, and I asked her to wait a moment, during which time I turned on my dictaphone.

"That's not fair," she said.

"Don't worry. No one else will ever hear this tape. I will give it to you and you may destroy it."

"Yes, but you're going to play it back to me."

"So what?"

"You just want me to hear myself because I sound so juvenile."

"If you know that as a mature young woman you should not be reacting in a juvenile manner, then just stop the juvenile stuff and react like the mature person you are."

This woman gained valuable insight, essentially on her own. The realization that her anger was a juvenile expression helped her to realize she was approaching other issues in her life in a juvenile manner as well.

Much the same can be achieved by writing down all your feelings and then reading what you have written, preferably aloud. You may then be able to do away with the feelings of anger or frustration that have impaired your sound judgment.

Now pick up the pen again and write whatever solutions come to mind. You may have thought to quit your job because your employer was rude and unfair, or to tell your parents that you will never, ever set foot in their house again because of how they treated you, or to send your engagement ring back to your fiancé because of something he said or did. And, by the way, include the possibility of going down to the store and getting a half gallon of ice cream. Write down all your options, then reread them.

You see, thought is both emotional and rational. When our feelings and our reasoning are in harmony, we are usually on the right track. Problems occur when our reason says one thing and our emotions say something else. Often our emotions are so intense that they obscure our rational thought. By putting our feelings and possible solutions in writing, we give our intellect an opportunity to break loose from the stranglehold of our emotions, and we can make better judgments. It is very likely that you will be able to exercise your rational capacities and decide that eating the half gallon of ice cream will not improve the situation with your job, parents, or boyfriend.

Chapter Twenty-One

Bringing in the Good Self

That two things cannot occupy the same space at the same time is a scientific principle that we can readily understand. A good self-image cannot exist as long as the bad self-image is present. We must make space for the good image, and that means sending the bad self packing.

This is not easy, but it is not as difficult as it seems. Setting aside the food problem for a moment, take paper and pencil and make a list of things you would like to change about yourself. For example:

- I would like to mingle more with people.

- I don't want to cower in my employer's presence.

- I want to be able to say no when I want to say no.

- I want to be able to express my opinions without feeling stupid.

- I don't want other people to make my choices for me.

- I don't want other people to feel sorry for me.

As with the diary, this list does not have to be completed in one sitting. You may do it over a period of days.

Now make a firm resolution that these undesirable features must go. It will take time, and you still have to find the method, but there is no turning back.

Making the list is an important first step. If you are remodeling your kitchen, you make a diagram of where you want the cabinets, the sink, the stove, the refrigerator, the microwave, the telephone, etc. Once you have a plan, you can proceed with the remodeling. The self-image is no different. And just as with remodeling the kitchen, you must get rid of what exists in order to make room for the new furnishings, so in "remodeling" your self-image, you should make a list of what you want to divest yourself of and then a list of "what I would like to be."

The things you own and keep are either functional or ornamental. Thus, if you have a beautiful grandfather clock that no longer keeps time, you may retain it as an attractive piece of furniture. On the other hand, if your can opener no longer works, you throw it in the garbage. It has no decorative purpose, and with its function gone, it is worthless.

What is it that gives us value? Few of us can claim that we are decorative, and if we do happen to be unusually attractive, this is a feature that is certain to diminish with time. Our value, then, lies in our function. But just what is our function? To eat, drink, and amuse ourselves in whatever way possible? Granted that we work in order to live, but what is the purpose in living?

One person may have a goal of working to preserve the environment. Another person may have a goal of community service. Another person may have a religious goal. Whatever the goal, it should be something other than self-gratification.

It is not even essential that we decide on a goal. What is uniquely human is our capacity to *think* about an ultimate purpose. Even if we have not found a goal, we can have a sense of value in searching for that goal and working toward it when we find it.

Although you may have a concept of what you want your new kitchen to look like, you would probably enlist the help of someone who has experience designing and remodeling kitchens. He or she may point out why a particular arrangement is not good and why another arrangement would be more attractive and more efficient. Similarly, in remodeling our self-image, it is best to enlist the help of an expert: a therapist.

Finding a therapist who can help with your self-image problem should not be too difficult, but neither can you assume that all therapists are equally good for this. My initial training as a psychiatrist was with a psychoanalytic orientation, but I have since found that approach to be of limited value. Too much emphasis is placed on the past, and while there is no denying the importance of past events and the impact they have on us today, there is nothing we can do about the past. It has been appropriately said, "Because the past is so important, you should take care of what you do in the past." Nor am I impressed that insight into the past makes all that much difference. A much more practical approach is contained in the statement, "Maybe your parents made you what you are, but if you stay that way, it's your own darn fault."

We have become more sophisticated medically, and we make inquiries about a doctor's treatment approach. Does he or she treat medically rather than surgically, and if surgically, does he or she use laser techniques when possible? We should use similar sophistication when choosing a psychotherapist and inquire whether his or her approach is primarily oriented toward elevating our self-esteem. Psychologists who belong to the cognitive school are particularly appropriate for self-esteem enhancement.

The problem with dwelling excessively on the past is that we are likely to place blame instead of seeking to make changes. It is much easier to feel sorry for ourselves as the victims of the unchangeable past than to initiate and effect changes in ourselves. For example, if you have low self-esteem you may be reluctant to ask for a raise or try for a promotion because of the risk of being turned down or failing. It is easier to see yourself as a victim of an employer who is exploiting you and of a system that does not permit your advancement. Granted that you may have developed such negative feelings because of early life experiences, but gaining insight into the sources of these feelings is not likely to contribute to your changing yourself. Rather, you must be helped and encouraged to take the necessary steps to advance yourself and accept the risk that your efforts may indeed be frustrated, in which case there is no option but to try again.

I once visited a salmon fishery on the Pacific Ocean. It is fascinating to watch how the salmon swim upstream, exerting much energy to swim against the flow. When they reach a cascade, they swim around a bit, then jump to the higher level. If they do not succeed, they swim around a bit and try again, repeating the process until they succeed.

The salmon has a biologic instinct to reach a prede-termined goal, and it therefore swims against the tide and leaps up waterfalls, undeterred by failure. A human being's goal should be intellectual rather than instinctive, but once we set a goal, we should be ready to swim upstream, overcome obstacles, and repeat our efforts until we succeed.

A person who considers herself inadequate may seek the comfort of associating with people of her level or even with those of a lesser caliber. Associating with people who are more skillful and knowledgeable may be uncomfortable, but they are the ones who can provide the initiative to improve yourself.

We all have sources of strength that are untapped and remain so unless something forces us to develop them. The heroic recovery of the actress Patricia Neal, which was dramatized on television, is an excellent example. Having suffered a disabling stroke, her family refused to cater to her, and she had to painfully exert herself to get whatever or to wherever she wanted. This resulted in her developing untapped resources and eventually returning to normal functioning. "Helping" her would have caused her to remain an invalid. Of course, we must be guided by experts who can establish that there are indeed resources that can be developed, for otherwise it would be cruel to demand the impossible of a person with limitations. Insofar as our emotional and intellectual resources are concerned, most people have abundant resources that are undeveloped, and a skilled therapist can help in their development.

From childhood on we have been behaving in a way to elicit approval from others, and this is only normal. When an infant takes his first step, which for him is a formidable challenge, it is common for the parents to express their joy, and this encourages him to proceed in the new method of ambulation, albeit fraught with the risk of falling and not being as safe as crawling on all fours. Many behavior patterns that begin in childhood are reinforced or extinguished by how people react to them, and this continues throughout our formative years. It is important that we recognize this, because not all of the behaviors that others desire of us are necessarily good for us. Some people encourage our behaviors because they are to *their* best advantage. Doing too much of what others would like us to do results in a less than optimum adjustment to life.

On the other hand, sometimes we develop a defiant attitude and rebel against what others expect of us. This is easily observed in young children. A defiance for the sake of defiance may result in rejecting some very constructive behaviors, although we rationalize our actions and delude ourselves that we have good reason for doing so.

When we react in compliance with others or in defiance of others, we are essentially allowing other people to determine how we act, and instead of being our own person, we are what other people make us. This is virtually inevitable in our early years of life, and that is what is meant by, "You may be what your parents made you, but if you stay that way it's your own darn fault." At some point in life we should take a good look at ourselves and begin to think, "What would I really want for myself?"

While it is not easy to convince yourself that the self-concept you have been harboring for several decades is erroneous, and it is certainly not easy to change behavior patterns that have become deeply ingrained, both of these tasks become less difficult if you understand that the self-image and the behavior patterns are the consequences of the opinions of others rather than your own. If you can conclude, "It is time that I become what I want to be rather than what others expect of me," there is greater motivation to make the necessary changes.

If you have become what you are by doing things that elicit the approval of others, then any changes you make may result in the disapproval of others. "What has gotten into Jane?" they may say. You must be ready to withstand the reaction of others.

Putting yourself first does not mean you can ignore the needs of others, but you really cannot have a healthy self-image if you are constantly driven by what others expect of you. You should indeed be considerate of the feelings of others and help them understand why you must make certain changes in yourself.

For example, Frank was always a good boy who sought to please his parents. When he got married, his mother continued to expect him to address her needs first. Frank's wife did not wish to play second fiddle and felt that his first allegiance was to her and the children. He was free to do whatever he could for his mother after his obligations to his family were met. Frank was caught in a dilemma, where he would disappoint either his wife or his mother, and his weight of more than three hundred pounds was the result of his eating away his frustrations. In therapy, Frank came to realize that what he wanted to do and what he should do was care for his family's needs first, and he had to gently explain to his mother why he had to change his behavior.

Various other changes may be necessary as you examine your actions and discover what it is that you are doing out of reaction to others' wishes. There is no need to make precipitous changes. A self-actualization does not occur overnight; it may take several years to achieve this. However, you should have a general plan about what you want to accomplish, and you can modify this plan as you proceed.

Chapter Twenty-Two

The Therapeutic Group

For compulsive-eating problems, group therapy is generally more effective than individual therapy. There may occasionally be a need for one or more individual sessions, especially when you do not feel comfortable discussing some highly charged emotional issue in a group, but on the whole, the group process is more effective.

Although every compulsive eater knows that there are millions of others like herself, this does not stop her from feeling that she is in some ways very different and that no one else has experienced her particular emotional stresses and dilemma. The group experience helps dissolve these feelings of loneliness and estrangement, as it becomes evident that whatever your individual circumstances, there is nevertheless much commonality in the emotional reactions they evoke, and no one is really all that unique.

The compulsive eater may read in books or hear in lectures that food has become a substitute for relationships and have this pointed out to her in one-to-one therapy. Yet this remains essentially an intellectual insight that does not effect any change. When you see this mechanism operate in other people, it is much easier to grasp that it is really so, and after identifying the process in others, you can much more easily apply it to yourself.

Another advantage of the group is that it helps initiate the shift from unhealthy to healthy dependency. As a rule, dependence on a single person is much more likely to become problematic than dependence on a group. We are all dependent on the community as a whole to do things that we cannot do ourselves, and the community is not likely to develop such intense involvement in us as to become unhealthy codependents. Individual therapy is fraught with the risk of the patient shifting her dependency onto the therapist, and although a skillful therapist is alert to this and can help the patient overcome this tendency and become self-sufficient, it is not unusual for even a good therapist to fall into the trap and become pathologically codependent, taking on personal responsibility for the patient's recovery.

Some compulsive eaters are so needy that their demands on the therapist are impossible to satisfy. This may result in termination of treatment. In a therapeutic group these demands are spread out and diluted, because no one person needs to be the provider for the many needs of any individual. The excessive neediness can thus be discussed and managed much easier than in one-to-one therapy.

I know of one physician who was a "guardian angel" for his patients, allowing them to call him whenever the need arose. He then made the mistake of dying, and most of his patients promptly relapsed. This was an unhealthy dependency-codependency, and this can be more easily averted by group therapy.

152

Another bit of intellectual insight of limited value is that compulsive eaters do not eat for hunger but because of some emotional distress that is alleviated by food. This is no doubt true, because real hunger is an expression of the body's need for nourishment. Any craving for food beyond that is technically not "hunger." Yet, when compulsive eaters go to the refrigerator, they may not be able to separate this craving from the sensation of hunger. This important distinction between hunger in the head and hunger in the stomach is much more easily achieved by the description and exchanges within the group, and once the true nature of the craving is identified, and especially its relationship to certain emotions and triggers, detaching it from food and substituting food with a much more appropriate behavior is easier.

Over and above the actual consumption of food, compulsive eaters are preoccupied with thinking about food, even when not eating. They can easily spend hours planning meals and then reading up on diets. Food can essentially take over the entire personality. It is probably true that the human mind can never be completely blank, and when the average person is not concentrating on anything in particular, her mind can wander to any one of many topics, and she can rather easily direct her thoughts to any topic she wants. Not so with compulsive eaters. When not actively engaged in something that demands their conscious attention, compulsive eaters' minds do not wander at all but make a beeline for food, and they are quite helpless in directing it elsewhere. This preoccupation and techniques to overcome it are more effectively dealt with in group.

In a compulsive-eating therapy group, there is greater possibility of recognizing the fallacy of "If only I were thinner, everything would be fine." This is a familiar resistance to change that occurs in one-to-one therapy, with the patient displacing everything onto the excessive weight. In a group, where there are likely to be people who are only minimally overweight yet have the same feelings as those who weigh much more, the weight issue may be defused. A woman who is eighty pounds overweight may tell the therapist, "If I were able to lose sixty pounds I would be in heaven," but when she sees and hears another woman who is ten pounds above her ideal weight voice the same complaints, this tends to expose the weight issue as being an artifact and helps place proper focus on the real, emotional issues that underlie the problem. This is even more so if there is a bulimic in the group who is at or even below her ideal weight and presents essentially the same feelings. The importance of the body image and of the fantasy self becomes much more evident.

A therapy group may resemble the family structure, with the therapist being the parent and the patients being the children. Since many of the emotional conflicts of compulsive eaters involve either child-parent difficulties or sibling relationship problems, the group provides an arena where these feelings can be brought to life, and a skilled therapist can guide the patients out of the maze of emotional feelings that resulted from problematic family interactions. Some therapists who are trained in Gestalt techniques or psychodrama, which allow people to act out their feelings in the protective confines of the group, are particularly adept in flushing out emotions that are having paralytic effects.

Earlier I noted that eating-dieting and bingeing-purging may represent conflicting attitudes that compulsive eaters act out, perhaps compliance versus defiance, passivity versus aggression, or femininity versus masculinity. These polar opposites are likely to be more evident in group therapy, as compulsive eaters manifest these conflicting feelings in the group interaction. Once identified, they can be resolved, and with their resolution, their manifestation and pathologic eating may disappear.

In addition to the various factors that are directly involved in the compulsive-eating pattern, many self-esteem issues are more easily identified and resolved in group therapy. It is typical that a person who is unable to recognize that she has an erroneous negative self-concept easily recognizes this in someone else and comments to the other person, "Why do you think that way about yourself?" She is likely to point out the positives of which the other person seems to be unaware, and that the poor self-image is a fantasy. As the bad fantasy self is present in every compulsive eater, every group member can identify it in the other members of the group, which makes it much easier for her to begin to accept that her own self-concept is a fantasy, and this opens the way for attaining a true self-awareness and a positive self-concept.

In summary, group therapy offers the most effective method for dealing with both the direct and indirect causes of compulsive eating, and it is highly recommended as a major component of recovery.

Chapter Twenty-Three

Self-Help Groups

A therapy group consists of a fixed number of people who meet regularly with a therapist to deal with specific issues, some of which were described in the previous chapter. The therapist can bring to light important psychological factors of which you are unaware and, in particular, can direct attention to the crucial problems of relationships and self-esteem that are at the core of compulsive eating. A self-help group is a support group where people with similar problems can pool their strengths and assist one another. It is less structured than a therapy group and operates on its own without a group leader. While a psychotherapist may offer valuable insights and understanding, the practical wisdom provided by a layperson who has "been there" is invaluable.

Beetle Bailey. Reprinted with special permission of King Features Syndicate.

Attendance and composition of the self-help group may fluctuate. You make many contacts within the group and thus have a greater number of people upon whom to draw for assistance, and you also have the opportunity to provide assistance to others. Groups such as Overeaters Anonymous (OA) are ubiquitous, which provides the additional advantage of having a resource available virtually anywhere in the world, wherever you are on business or pleasure.

The twelve-step program of Overeaters Anonymous, like Alcoholics Anonymous (AA), can be effective if it is put in proper perspective. One recovering alcoholic with many years of sobriety says, "If your problem is alcohol, you don't need AA. My problem wasn't alcohol, it was alcoho*lism,* and when I stopped drinking, I still had the 'ism' to deal with." Those who expect the program to teach them control may find it less effective. Those who look upon themselves as having an "ism" and wishing to use the twelve-step program to deal with the "ism," may find it much more helpful, but this requires personal and spiritual (though not necessarily religious) commitment.

So in addition to the work done on acquiring a valued self-image in the therapy group, dimension can be added by the self-help group, particularly a twelve-step group. Let us look at the twelve steps of OA:

1. We admitted we were powerless over food—that our lives had become unmanageable.

2. Came to believe that a power greater than ourselves could restore us to sanity.

3. Made a decision to turn our will and our lives over to the care of God *as we understood Him.*

4. Made a searching and fearless moral inventory of ourselves.

5. Admitted to God, to ourselves, and to another human being the exact nature of our wrongs.

6. Were entirely ready to have God remove all these defects of character.

7. Humbly asked Him to remove our shortcomings.

8. Made a list of all persons we had harmed and became willing to make amends to them all.

9. Made direct amends to such people wherever possible, except when to do so would injure them or others.

10. Continued to take personal inventory and when we were wrong, promptly admitted it.

11. Sought through prayer and meditation to improve our conscious contact with God *as we understood Him,* praying only for knowledge of His will for us and the power to carry that out.

12. Having had a spiritual awakening as the result of these steps, we tried to carry this message to compulsive overeaters and to practice these principles in all our affairs.

In the first three steps you do away with the vexing issue of trying to implement the "automatic" control, the shutoff mechanism that turns off the appetite when the body's nutritional requirements have been satisfied, which is obviously not functional in the compulsive eater. That is all that is meant by "powerlessness." Given the lack of the automatic shutoff, you recognize the need for some other method of control, which is what is meant by "a power greater than ourselves." The concept in step 3 is that you must find a goal outside of yourself, so that eating no longer occupies a place of prominence in or totally monopolizes your life.

The twelve-step program originated with the Oxford Group, comprised of people who espoused religious ideas. However, the program is used by people who do not have a religious orientation and even by atheists. The concept of "turning one's will over to God as I understand Him" may simply mean finding something to live for other than gratifying your own desires. This is desirable not only for the alcoholic or compulsive eater but also for every human being. Properly understood, the third step directs you away from self-centeredness and total absorption with yourself, which is characteristic of the compulsive eater.

Steps 4 and 5 are the core of self-awareness, and properly done they enable you to divest yourself of character defects and develop your character strengths. The inventory referred to in step 4 should be just that, an inventory. If you were considering purchasing a business concern, you would desire a thorough inventory, which consists of knowing both the assets and liabilities of the business. Similarly, a personal inventory means recognizing your character strengths as well as your character defects.

Steps 6 and 7 might appear to be relevant only to those who have a religious orientation and appeal to a deity for help. But this is not necessarily so. If you think of a power greater than yourself as being a therapy group or a self-help group, you may enlist the help of these groups in divesting yourself of character defects. Steps 8 and 9 are of crucial importance in overcoming resentments and divesting yourself of guilt feelings, which can gnaw away at you and trigger compulsive eating. While pathologic guilt feelings that have no validity in reality should be dealt with in therapy, there are guilt feelings that are reality based and that result from misdeeds you have done. Steps 8 and 9 eliminate these and are extremely helpful in relieving you of a significant emotional burden.

Step 10 ought to be obvious—but it isn't. Most of us as children tried to cover up our mistakes. We put the pieces of our mother's broken vase in the trash and hoped she wouldn't notice that the vase had disappeared. It didn't work then, and it doesn't work now. The long-term effects of denying our mistakes are invariably detrimental. We can save an enormous amount of energy by promptly admitting our mistakes and not defending them. Furthermore, we gain in self-esteem and stature by owning up to and apologizing for our mistakes.

As with steps 6 and 7, step 11 does not have to be restricted to a deity. If you do not believe in God but establish goals in life outside of your immediate self-gratification and adopt some power greater than yourself as your guide and mentor, you can implement step 11. Finally, step 12 consists of making yourself available to help others in their struggle with similar problems. Where all the pitfalls of codependency need to be recognized and avoided, you can gain healthy self-esteem by helping others.

Here is a letter from a woman who had a successful recovery from both alcoholism and bulimia:

First, I try to work the 12-step program of AA every day, especially applying the first three steps to my eating disorder.

Second, 90% of the time I stick to a food plan (which includes sugar and white flour) that has about 1,200 calories per day. When we're out or on vacation I eat whatever I want in moderation. The key is never to deny myself a certain food, thereby setting up a binge. By doing this I have lost 47 pounds and successfully kept it off for seven years.

Third, I do some sort of aerobic exercise— swim, walk, or step-aerobics 3–4 times a week without fail.

Combining these three elements and making them a part of my life is what works for me and is the only way I know.

Finally, a self-help group can be of infinite value in helping you deal with the occasional relapses that can occur during recovery. If you perceive a relapse as a total failure, your self-esteem is seriously eroded, and you tend to lose hope. If you recognize a relapse as an opportunity for further growth, wherein you can analyze what triggered the relapse and with the help of others in the group consider how to deal with such happenings if they recur, you can convert the relapse from a negative to a positive occurrence.

Chapter Twenty-Four

Can I Do It Myself?

Is it absolutely necessary to have therapy or participate in a support group? If you accept the premise that in order to recover from compulsive eating you must alter your self-image, can't you accomplish this on your own?

There is certainly no harm in trying. The track record of unaided personality changes is not the greatest, but there is nothing to lose in trying. The reason for the limited value of the do-it-yourself approach is that the distorted perception of the self that caused your negative self-image in the first place is likely to continue as long as you look at yourself through "lenses" that distort the image. Your self-perception tends to remain subjective, and as long as you are looking for the new self through the same lenses that caused the initial misperception, it is unlikely that you will find something much different. Furthermore, there are so many factors that cause us to maintain the status quo and to rationalize away many reasons for change, that without an objective observer to alert us to these misperceptions and rationalizations, we are likely to remain exactly where we were.

Nevertheless, you can try. There are some excellent books listed in the bibliography on how to attain self-esteem and correct an erroneous self-concept. Reading these and giving serious thought to their content and applying the information to yourself may impress you sufficiently that you begin to make some changes. It is important, however, not to get bogged down in theories. We can have a great deal of intellectual insight and yet not change our behavior one iota. Progress can be made only by action, by implementing the recommendations toward self-esteem enhancement.

Paper and pencil are helpful tools. An unexpressed thought is of little value, and generally people do not talk to themselves. Writing down the ideas you gather from reading and from introspection and writing down how you plan to translate these concepts into action are more likely to result in constructive change than simply meditating. As you write down the changes you want to make, include a reasonable target date for achieving them—not tomorrow, but not ten years from now either. When the target arrives, reevaluate how much of the goal you have achieved, and if you have not achieved it, examine the obstacles that prevented progress.

One of the greatest hindrances to self-actualization is concealing feelings. Earlier I alluded to the fact that in a dysfunctional family, the cardinal rule is "don't talk." This pattern of concealment can occur within an individual just as well as within a family, and the result is that part of yourself remains sequestered, unexamined, and disowned. There is then part of yourself that is a "monster" hidden away in the closet, and this sequestration and disowning of yourself impedes the development of full self-awareness.

163

It is therefore helpful to have pencil and paper handy, and when feelings arise, whatever they are, take the first opportunity to write them down.

While the feelings are still fresh in your mind, write down the incidents that brought them about. Write down your reaction to the incident or to the feelings, then write down what you might do to avoid such incidents and feelings if they are stressful, or how to reinforce them if they are pleasant. There is no need to save these notes, and after reading the paper a few times you may get rid of it.

In addition to the various goals we seek for ourselves, we should work on an ultimate goal. What do we expect to do with our lives? This may require a bit of philosophizing and reading, and you do not have to come up

164

with an immediate answer. Much of the value in pursuing an ultimate goal is precisely in its pursuit, as you reject spurious goals that are momentarily pleasant but of no lasting value.

Maintaining a proper state of self-esteem is difficult for someone who has been harboring a negative concept for years. It is therefore helpful to combat this attitude with positive affirmations. There are numerous books with daily affirmations, some of a religious character, others not. It is an excellent practice to read a brief affirmation several times a day.

Both positive and negative attitudes tend to propagate themselves. If we are in a negative state of mind, we may say negative things and act negatively, which then sets the stage for more negativity. The reverse is true of positivity, which is why even a brief period of positive thinking that results from reading an affirmation can set into motion a positive chain reaction. Some of these books are directed at specific problems, such as alcoholism, drug addiction, incest survivors, adult children of alcoholics, sexual addiction, etc. However, all contain messages of affirmation that can be of benefit to everyone.

It is also advisable to recite affirmations to yourself such as:

- I am a good, worthy person.

- I am a likable person.

- I can control whether I feel good or bad.

- I accept my body the way it is but will try to make it even healthier.

- Food is a nutrient.

- Food can be only as powerful as I allow it to be.

- I can be free of problem eating.

- I don't have to prove myself.

- I can say no when I think it is proper to say no.

- I can forgive myself for my mistakes.

These and other statements, said aloud to yourself, in the overall context of working on your self-esteem, can have an impact.

You may enhance your self-help program by sharing your thoughts and feelings with a like-minded friend. One woman I know calls her best friend every Friday to discuss their progress and lack of progress, share tips, and encourage each other. They have their ups and downs, but neither has gotten close to their all-time high weights. While this is not quite group therapy, a "buddy system" that allows you to express your feelings and get feedback can be invaluable.

Chapter Twenty-Five

Some Practical Suggestions

I began this book by denouncing miracle diets as counterproductive. This does not mean that there is no place for a diet. To the contrary, it is important to have a proper diet, but it should not be a self-defeating, quick-fix diet. Furthermore, although a proper diet is essential, the primary focus should not be on the food, but on yourself.

You can get very reliable information for a reasonable, sustainable, weight-reduction program by consulting a competent dietician. The dietician at your local hospital or health club is usually an excellent resource person, and your physician may help you get an appointment. Your hospital may provide classes on nutrition and weight reduction. These are often free of charge or at a low cost. Regardless of how much weight you wish to lose, there is no need to do this rapidly. The body does not tolerate sudden changes well, and if you want to take off thirty pounds, you will do much better if you give yourself six or seven months to reach your goal.

Adhering to a proper diet does not require weighing every portion of food. If you have no idea of how much an "average" portion is, a "large" apple or a "medium" potato, your dietician may help you estimate these. If you do use a food scale, put it away after the first month. Being obsessive-compulsive about limiting the size of your portions is almost as bad as compulsive eating.

You're going to have to make some difficult changes. For example, it is important that you separate eating from other activities, such as watching television or talking on the phone to a friend. Also, don't gobble your food. Chew it and give yourself a chance to savor the taste. As I pointed out earlier, some compulsive eaters swallow their food without chewing it, and not only do they actually fail to enjoy what they are eating but they also thereby interfere with important phases of digestion, which are set into motion by proper chewing. Little wonder that they end up with heartburn, gas, and bloating.

Sit down at the table to eat. Don't eat while standing, and don't eat while driving the car or walking down the hall. Give yourself a chance to finish a mouthful before picking up the next fork- or spoonful. The food on your plate is not going to run away. But you say you're impatient? Learning patience is an important aspect of recovery.

It is helpful to put all your food for the meal on one plate, rather than taking it in bits or pieces. Also, avoid seconds. And if you remember your mother's reprimand for leaving food on your plate because "just think of the starving children in China or Ethiopia," this is one time you may neglect your mother's teachings. There is no logical reason to feel guilty. The starving children will not be helped by your cleaning your plate.

Finally, force yourself to sit at the table for a few minutes after you have finished your meal. I know you are under pressure of time, but you will more than make up for these few moments by gradually learning how to relax.

You may think that these changes are impossible to achieve and that you will go crazy if you try. All changes in habits are difficult, but with a bit of patience and perseverance, the awkwardness disappears. Invest just thirty consecutive days in these new patterns of eating, and you will find that they become second nature. You may have already spent months and years and a lot of money trying to lose weight, only to end up with repeated disappointments. This time you don't have to invest any money, just a trial of thirty days. Give yourself a break. You deserve it.

Throughout this book I have placed great emphasis on the self-image and the need for obtaining a positive self-image in order to maintain the recovery of an eating problem. While the psychological attitude is of utmost importance, there are several other ingredients that should accompany psychological changes. As with the attainment of a self-image, these too require determination, time, and effort. If you have read this far, you have undoubtedly already concluded that achieving and maintaining weight reduction is not going to be easy. The easy ways are the ones I enumerated and eliminated in chapter 1.

Exercise is a most important component, and it is necessary to plan, make, and adhere to an exercise schedule. First have an evaluation by your physician to make certain that there is no restriction against exercising, and then exercise *without interruption* for thirty minutes three times a week. Exercise may consist of jogging, swimming, rowing, walking, bicycling, aerobics, or any other energetic activity, and it should be performed at a pace that works up a sweat. If possible, exercise with a partner. Schedule exercise time and give it priority. Don't yield to any of the many rationalizations for not exercising.

If you are on your way out to exercise and the phone rings, let it ring! You can reduce the boredom by playing music or listening to books on tape during exercise. One person I know has listened to all of Charles Dickens while on the treadmill and now is starting Jane Austen.

Chew your food instead of gobbling it. Chewing your food slows your eating but also increases your enjoyment by allowing you to taste your food instead of swallowing it virtually whole.

Reward yourself. Think of something you have been delaying until you lose weight, for example, going to the swimming pool or accepting a date. Certainly you will do these things *after* you have lost weight, but don't make everything contingent on weight loss. Do something now! It may be difficult for you to appear in a bathing suit when you think of yourself as fat, but do it anyway. You will be pleased to discover that the only one who thinks negatively of your body is *you.*

Acupuncture, biofeedback, hypnosis, or imaging may help relieve anxiety and tension, and they may diminish the craving for food. If done properly, these may help provide some "manual" control in place of the dysfunctional "automatic" control mechanism. The pitfall in these is that you may rely on them as being magic cures rather than helpful adjuncts. Anything seen as a magic cure is counterproductive and is in the same category as any of the miracle diets whose inefficiency has been established. If you adopt the rather strenuous course of making the necessary changes in yourself by increased self-awareness, therapy and support groups, exercise, and working with a reputable dietician, and then want to use one or more of these methods as adjuncts, there is nothing wrong with that.

What about weight-loss clinics that are under medical management and supervision? The problem with these is that we often have an image of doctors as miracle workers, who have potent medications and surgical procedures that can do anything except resurrect the dead. The desire for rapid and dramatic results, particularly the lure of having someone else do the work and relieve you of the efforts of a demanding weight-loss regimen that requires character changes, may combine with the image of the physician as being a miracle worker. The danger is that you may neglect all the essential changes I have described and rely on the medical treatment to bring about the desired result. The actual result will be a fairly rapid weight loss with eventual return of the pounds. This is evident in many cases of surgical bypass, stapling of the stomach, insertion of balloons into the stomach, and various other techniques.

Chapter Twenty-Six

The Fullness of Our Humanity

I once was talking with a patient about the importance of self-esteem, when he interrupted me. "How can you expect me to have any self-esteem?" he asked. He went on to describe many incidents in his life that had made him feel worthless. I asked him if he had ever seen an exhibit of jewels, in which there was, say, a diamond pin with a ten-karat perfect blue-white jewel, worth hundreds of thousands of dollars.

"Do you know what that diamond looked like when it was brought out of the mine? It looked like a dirty piece of glass, with no beauty whatsoever. Most people would have discarded it as worthless. Fortunately, an expert examined the ore, and he knew that inside this unattractive, dirty rock there was a priceless gem. The stone was then processed, until the scintillating diamond emerged. No one can put any beauty into a dirty rock. All the processing plant can do is remove the material that is concealing the beauty that lies within.

"Don't you tell me that you are worthless," I said. "I happen to be the expert who knows that there is great beauty within you. What we must do is help you get rid of whatever it is that is covering up that beauty, so that both you and others can appreciate it."

People are the jewel of creation. Each of us has inestimable beauty and worth, but at times we fail to see and appreciate it because it is covered up.

Human beings are different from and superior to lower forms of life in more ways than one. While we do have a greater intellect than animals, our superiority as humans is not a function only of a higher IQ. There are a number of features that give us our distinction.

People are capable of learning lessons from the experiences of the past, even from past generations, and to avoid repeating destructive behavior.

People are capable of thinking about goals and purposes in life, whereas animals do not have any ultimate goals and are driven only by their instinctive and physical desires.

People are capable of thinking about how to improve themselves and consciously and volitionally to make salutary changes in themselves. People are thus able to grow in character, whereas animals grow primarily only in size. Salutary changes that do occur in animals, as when a caterpillar turns into a beautiful butterfly, are programmed into the animal's genes and are not brought about by the animal's conscious desire to improve itself.

People are capable of thinking about the long-term consequences of their actions. Animals are motivated by impulse and cannot deny gratifying a physical urge on the basis of long-term consequences.

People are capable of delaying gratifications of a desire until more appropriate times. Animals react to an impulse with action to bring about immediate gratification and cannot defer gratification.

People can make moral and ethical decisions and are thus not under the domination and tyranny of their physical urges. Animals might be stopped from gratifying a desire by fear of punishment, but they cannot make moral or ethical decisions that would frustrate a bodily urge. Hence, human beings are the only living creatures that can be said to be truly free and not slaves to their bodily demands.

To be fully human, then, we must implement these capacities that are distinctive features of our humanity. Failure to do so lessens our uniqueness as humans. We can hardly be in possession of a good self when we are lacking the uniqueness and distinctions of humanity.

Let us see what happens when you are subject to the compulsion of destructive eating habits.

You do not benefit or learn from the history of the past. Rather, you repeat patterns that have been failures, deluding yourself that "this time will be different." You may have tried various crash diets or weight-losing gimmicks only to find that they were worthless and that the lost weight was quickly regained, yet you repeat this futile behavior, ignoring the lessons of the past.

The purpose of life for a compulsive eater is centered around food and weight. The goal of losing weight becomes the central theme in life, displacing everything else. Your mind becomes totally occupied with food, diets, schedules, etc., leaving no room for contemplation of ultimate goals.

Compulsive eating is detrimental to both physical and emotional health. Self-improvement is not feasible when you are essentially engaged in self-deterioration.

Compulsive eaters are obviously unable to consider

the long-term consequences of their actions, succumbing instead to the impulse of the moment. Even if you are aware that you will regret yielding to the craving for food, this does not deter you from doing so.

Compulsive eaters are generally unable to delay their eating, and when they crave food they eat anywhere and everywhere, as soon as possible.

By definition, *compulsive* eaters are not free, being subject to the tyranny of their compulsion. They may rationalize why they eat, but the fact is that they eat because they feel helpless to resist the drive.

We can see that the very features that make us completely human and give us the distinction of being superior to lower forms of life undergo erosion in compulsive eating. As long as such erosion continues, it is difficult for a good self to replace the bad fantasy self.

Acquisition or restoration of self-esteem requires exercising all our unique human capabilities. We may institute these in regard to other areas of life as well as food and eating, and then gradually increase these strengthened traits more and more to involve food, so that we do learn from the past, develop goals in life that are not food-oriented, seek to improve ourselves both physically and psychologically, delay gratification, consider our actions in light of future consequences, and finally, throw off the enslavement of compulsion as we take pride in the freedom to exercise mind over matter. This allows for the emergence of the truly and fully human being, the crown jewel of creation, that is contained within us.

It may seem to be a catch-22 that you cannot overcome compulsive eating habits unless you develop a concept of a good self, but you cannot develop a good self-concept unless you have overcome the compulsion. The fact is, however, that as soon as you begin to make the effort, the conquest begins. One recovering alcoholic described his recovery in the following picturesque manner: "It was like standing on the shore, waiting to get across the river, when two guys come along and say, 'You want to get across the river? Start rowing!' 'But there is no boat,' I said. 'Never mind,' they said. 'Start rowing and the boat will appear.' I thought they were crazy, but since I had no choice, I started rowing, and sure enough, the boat did appear."

The same can be said of compulsive eating. Begin to implement the distinctive human traits. Start rowing, and the boat will appear.

Appendix

My emphasis has been on making salutary changes in the *person* rather than in the *food*. Nevertheless, it is necessary to have some general guidelines on what constitutes a healthful diet, in contrast to a "miracle" diet. There are many variables that can affect the choice of a proper diet, and you should consult a dietician for establishing your specific dietary needs. What follows, then, is essentially a rule of thumb or very general dietary principles.

It is simplistic to dismiss calories as being insignificant, as some books on weight loss have suggested, although it is true that some foods "burn up" calories in the process of digestion and metabolism. It is necessary to calculate approximately how many calories you need.

If you want to maintain your weight, multiply your weight by 12 to arrive at an approximate amount of daily calories you should consume. For example, if you weigh 105 pounds, then you need about 1,260 calories (12 × 105) to maintain your weight. The caloric intake varies with the amount of exercise you do.

The next rule of thumb is that one pound equals approximately 3,500 calories. Suppose you weigh 150 pounds. You need 1,800 calories a day (12×150) to maintain your weight. If you decrease your intake by 300 calories a day, then you will lose about one pound in twelve days ($3,500 \div 300$). If you consume 1,300 calories a day, you should lose one pound in a week ($3500 \div 500 = 7$).

It is important to realize that the body does not adjust well to abrupt changes. If you lose four pounds a month, you can reduce your weight by twenty-four pounds in six months. You might wish to do so more rapidly, but whereas a more rapid loss of weight may appear dramatic to you, the body may consider it to be *traumatic* rather than dramatic. Therefore, choose a diet that is sustainable over the long term.

A well-balanced diet consists of three servings from the vegetable group, two servings from the milk group, two servings from the meat group, two servings from the fruit group, and six servings from the bread group. This should provide approximately 1,600 calories. If you desire a 1,200-calorie diet, simply decrease the portions, using three-fourths of a serving where a whole serving is called for.

Again, please remember that these are rule-of-thumb guidelines. I cannot emphasize strongly enough that you should have an individualized diet designed by a competent dietician. The dietary department of your local hospital is certain to have a dietician on staff whom you may consult.

Food Guide Pyramid

A Guide to Daily Food Choices

The **Food Guide Pyramid** emphasizes foods from the five food groups shown in the three lower sections of the pyramid.

Each of these food groups provides some, but not all, of the nutrients you need. Foods in one group can't replace those in another. No one food group is more important than another—for good health, you need them all.

The pyramid is an outline of what to eat each day. It's not a rigid prescription but a general guide that lets you choose a healthful diet that's right for you. The pyramid calls for eating a variety of foods to get the nutrients you need and at the same time the right amount of calories to maintain a healthy weight.

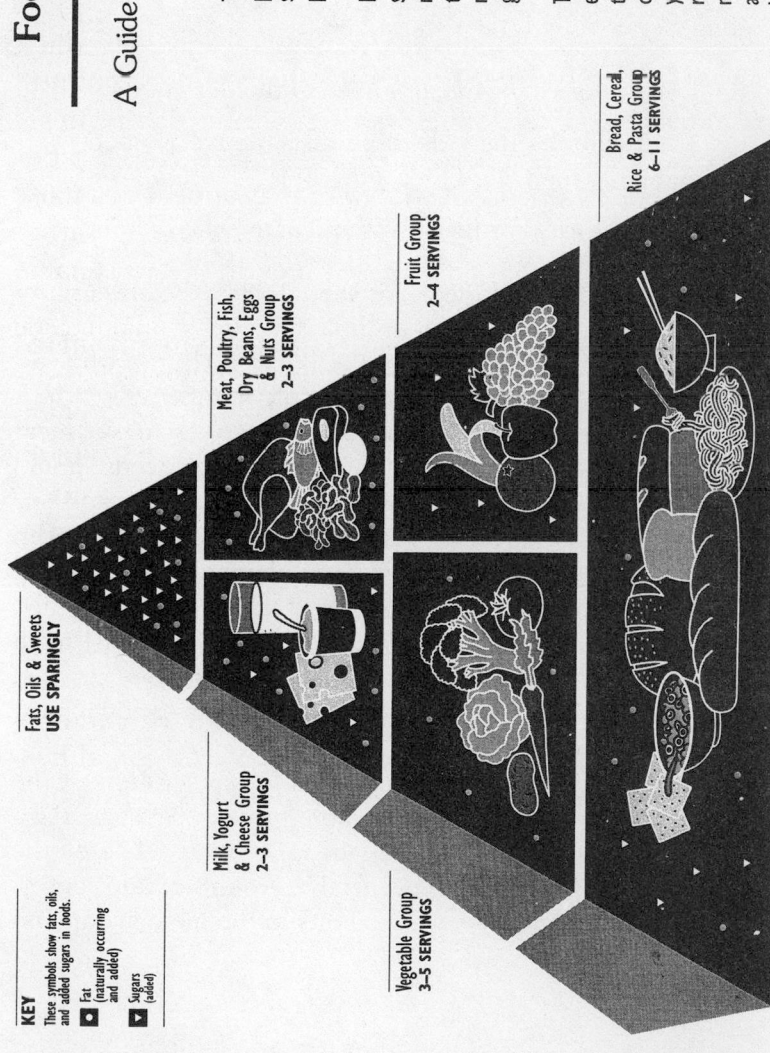

KEY
These symbols show fats, oils, and added sugars in foods.

◆ Fat (naturally occurring and added)

▼ Sugars (added)

Fats, Oils & Sweets
USE SPARINGLY

Milk, Yogurt & Cheese Group
2–3 SERVINGS

Meat, Poultry, Fish, Dry Beans, Eggs & Nuts Group
2–3 SERVINGS

Vegetable Group
3–5 SERVINGS

Fruit Group
2–4 SERVINGS

Bread, Cereal, Rice & Pasta Group
6–11 SERVINGS

How Many Servings Do You Need?

The Food Guide Pyramid shows a range of servings for each food group. The number of servings that are right for you depends on how many calories you need. Calories are a way to measure food energy. The energy your body needs depends on your age, sex, and size. It also depends on how active you are.

In general, daily intake should be:

- 1,600 calories for most women and older adults

- 2,200 calories for kids, teen girls, active women, and most men

- 2,800 calories for teen boys and active men

Those with lower calorie needs should select the lower number of servings from each food group. Their diet should include two servings of meat for a total of five ounces. Those with average calorie needs should select the middle number of servings from each food group. They should include two servings of meat for a total of six ounces. Those with higher calorie needs should select the higher number of servings from each food group. Their diet should include three servings of meat for a total of seven ounces. Also, pregnant or breast-feeding women, teens, or young adults up to age twenty-four should select three servings of milk.

The amount of food that counts as one serving is listed below. If you eat a larger portion, it is more than one serving. For example, a slice of bread is one serving, so a sandwich for lunch equals two servings.

For mixed foods, estimate the food group servings of the main ingredients. For example, a large piece of sausage pizza counts in the bread group (crust), the milk group (cheese), the meat group (sausage), and the vegetable group (tomato sauce). Likewise, a helping of beef stew counts in the meat group and the vegetable group.

What Counts as a Serving?

Bread, Cereal, Rice & Pasta Group

1 slice bread
1 tortilla
½ cup cooked rice, pasta, or cereal
1 ounce ready-to-eat cereal
½ hamburger roll, bagel, or English muffin
3–4 plain crackers (small)
1 pancake (4-inch)
½ croissant (large)
½ doughnut or danish (medium)
1/16 cake (average)
2 cookies (medium)
1/12 pie (2-crust, 8˝)

Meat, Poultry, Fish, Dry Beans, Eggs & Nuts Group

2½ to 3 ounces cooked lean beef, pork, lamb, veal, poultry, or fish

Count ½ cup cooked beans, 1 egg, 2 tablespoons peanut butter, or ⅓ cup nuts as 1 ounce of meat.

Milk, Yogurt & Cheese Group

1 cup milk or yogurt
1½ ounces natural cheese
2 ounces processed cheese
1½ cups ice cream or ice milk
1 cup frozen yogurt

Vegetable Group

½ cup chopped raw or cooked vegetables
1 cup raw, leafy vegetables
¾ cup vegetable juice
½ cup scalloped potatoes
½ cup potato salad
10 French fries

Fruit Group

1 piece fruit or melon wedge
¾ cup fruit juice
½ cup chopped, cooked, or canned fruit
¼ cup dried fruit

Fats, Oils & Sweets

use sparingly

181

Ideal Weight Range: Women

Height	Small Frame	Medium Frame	Large Frame
4'4"	93–98	96–108	105–118
4'5"	91–100	98–110	107–120
4'6"	93–102	100–112	109–122
4'7"	95–104	102–114	111–124
4'8"	97–106	104–116	113–126
4'9"	99–108	106–118	115–128
4'10"	100–110	108–120	117–131
4'11"	101–112	110–123	119–134
5'	103–115	112–126	122–137
5'1"	105–118	115–129	125–140
5'2"	108–121	118–132	128–144
5'3"	111–124	121–135	131–148
5'4"	114–127	124–138	134–152
5'5"	117–130	127–141	137–156
5'6"	120–133	130–144	140–160
5'7"	123–136	133–147	143–164
5'8"	126–139	136–150	146–167
5'9"	129–142	139–153	149–170
5'10"	132–145	142–156	152–173
5'11"	135–148	145–159	155–176

Ideal Weight Range: Men

Height	Small Frame	Medium Frame	Large Frame
4'7"	111–117	114–124	122–132
4'8"	113–119	116–126	124–134
4'9"	115–121	118–128	125–136
4'10"	117–123	119–130	127–138
4'11"	119–125	122–132	129–140
5'	121–127	124–134	131–142
5'1"	123–129	126–136	133–145
5'2"	125–131	128–138	135–148
5'3"	127–133	130–140	137–151
5'4"	129–135	132–143	139–155
5'5"	131–137	134–146	141–159
5'6"	133–140	137–149	144–163
5'7"	135–143	140–152	147–167
5'8"	137–146	143–155	150–171
5'9"	139–149	146–158	153–175
5'10"	141–152	149–161	156–179
5'11"	144–155	152–165	159–183
6'	147–159	155–169	163–187
6'1"	150–163	159–173	167–192
6'2"	153–167	162–177	171–197
6'3"	157–171	166–182	176–202

Bibliography

Branden, Nathaniel. *The Psychology of Self-Esteem*. New York: Bantam Books, 1971.

Hollis, Judi. *Fat and Furious*. New York: Ballantine Books, 1971.

———. *Fat Is a Family Affair*. Center City, MN: Hazelden, 1985.

L., Elisabeth. *Food for Thought*. Center City, MN: Hazelden, 1980.

Larsen, Ernie, and Carol Heggerty. *Believing in Myself*. New York: Simon & Schuster, 1991.

Satir, Virginia. *The New Peoplemaking*. Mountain View, VA: Science & Behavior Books, 1988.

Twerski, Abraham, M.D. *Life's Too Short!* New York: St. Martin's Press, 1995.